THE THIRD AGE

STORE

THE THIRD AGE

A Guide for Elderly People, Their Families and Friends

MURIEL SKEET

Foreword by David Hobman
Director, Age Concern England

Darton, Longman and Todd
London
Published in association with Age Concern England
and the Disabled Living Foundation

First published in Great Britain in 1982
by Darton, Longman and Todd Ltd
89 Lillie Road, London SW6 1UD

Published in association with
Age Concern England and the Disabled Living Foundation

ISBN 0 232 51484 4

British Library Cataloguing in Publication Data

Skeet, Muriel
  The third age.
  1. Old age
  I. Title
  305.2'6   HQ1061

  ISBN 0–232–51484–4

Phototypeset by Input Typesetting Ltd, London SW19 8DR
Printed in Great Britain by The Anchor Press Ltd and bound by
Wm Brendon & Son Ltd both of Tiptree, Essex.

The Men! O what venerable and reverend creatures did the aged seem! Immortal Cherubims! And young men glittering and sparkling Angels, and maids strange seraphic pieces of life and beauty! Boys and girls tumbling in the street, and playing, were moving jewels. I knew not that they were born or should die; but all things abided eternally as they were in their proper places.

from *Meditations on the Six Days of Creation*
Thomas Traherne 1717

CONTENTS

Foreword   ix
Preface   xi
Introduction   xiii

PART I: THE AGEING PROCESS

1 Ourselves and the Process of Ageing   3
2 Understanding the Process and Science of Ageing   10
3 A Brief Social and Economic Background to Ageing
   in the Eighties   19

PART II: MAINTAINING INDEPENDENCE

4 Deciding Where to Live   33
5 Controlling Financial and Legal Affairs   62
6 Continuing to be Oneself   78
7 Keeping Fit and Well   93
8 Restoring Function and Improving Ability   114

PART III: ACCEPTING DEPENDENCE

9   Running Risks and Having Rights   133
10 Caring for Someone Who is Very ill or is Dying   142
11 Being Practical When Bereaved   155

APPENDICES

1 Sources of General Information   167
2 Addresses of Some Agencies and Organizations   180
   Select Bibliography   204
   Index   215

Note

While every effort has been made by the author and the publishers to ensure that all material in this book is up-to-date, some details, especially in legal and financial areas, are liable to change. The appendixes at the back of the book provide a list of organizations which readers can consult for the latest detailed information on particular topics.

FOREWORD

It has rightly been said that enlightened self-interest is a most powerful motivating force for social change. The more we do to improve things for ourselves, the better it will be for everyone else as well. This principle applies just as much to our health as it does to our income. Prevention really is a great deal better than cure.

Sometimes, however, the barriers seem too formidable to overcome and there appears to be little, or nothing, which we can do individually to change our circumstances. We have to live within the body we have been given, and to make the most of the limited talents with which we have been endowed. We also have to accept the laws which other people make on our behalf as we do the decisions which those in authority make over the management of the economy or in the protection of the environment.

But no single professional has a monopoly in the problem-solving process, any more than professionals do in making sound judgements about how best to make the money go round or to preserve the countryside. There is a great deal which we can do for ourselves medically, socially and politically by intelligent, informed action.

In the case of ageing, we also need to adopt a positive and realistic approach to help us understand the nature of the process, and to recognize that it does impose certain restrictions; but also to see there are compensations against losses and ways to improve almost every conceivable kind of condition: but to do all this, we must have accurate information at our disposal, of the kind which is to be found in this excellent book by Muriel Skeet.

As readers will soon discover, the author shares her own wide knowledge with clarity and sensitivity, whether she is discussing areas which we often tend to avoid, such as sex and death, or whether she is concerned with purely practical matters such as where to go for specialized help.

Authors able to provide a wide range of information in single comprehensive volumes do a very considerable service. In the case of the *Third Age*, not only does Muriel Skeet pack her pages with a wealth of valuable information, she also has the ability of simplifying complex ideas, without diluting them, in ways which will make sense to both older people themselves as well as to those looking after them.

The *Third Age* makes it quite clear that whilst ageing is in essence a biological process, which cannot be reversed; it also has medical and social components which can be enhanced once we have exploded some of the more damaging myths about later life and removed those prejudices which stem from ignorance but which can lead to quite unnecessary unhappiness and discomfort.

David Hobman
Director,
Age Concern England

PREFACE

'Mr Salteena', wrote Daisy Ashford in *The Young Visiters*, 'was an elderly man of 42.'

While those of us who are either approaching or past that age may smile in wry amusement, in fact that young lady wrote something approaching the truth. We are all ageing from the time we are fully developed which is about the age of twenty or so; and at the time Miss Ashford wrote her delightful child masterpiece, a man of forty was well past the 'middle' of his life.

Few people in those days lived to 'a ripe old age'. Today there are, by Daisy Ashford's definition, many 'elderly' people and also very many very old people, living among, or sadly, more often than not, living apart from us. The proportion of persons aged eighty or more in the population is increasing every year. Today it is around the 26 million mark. By the year 2,000, only about twenty years or one generation away, it is estimated that there will be that number in that age group in developing countries alone.

The world is full of gloom and doom concerning many subjects and none more so than when contemplating this particular one. 'Too many people too old too soon,' we are told. 'There'll be no-one to look after them all in ten years' time,' declare our health and social service experts. Yet few people of sixty or even seventy require looking after now, a state which would have seemed impossible for people of that age even a few decades ago. By understanding and accepting old age, by planning and preparing for it, those of us who have not yet reached it can aim to need little looking after when we're eighty or even ninety. While there can be no blueprint to make old age the happiest time of our lives, a change of attitude towards it could work wonders.

This book is written for all those 'elderly men [and women] of forty-two' and for those under and over forty-two who are

aware of ageing. It is also written for all those who have
contact with any of these people. In short, it is written for
everyone, in an attempt to help them understand what is
happening to them and to others around them. It is hoped
that by understanding it a little more, old age will be enjoyed
a great deal more because it will be approached not as a
disease to be dreaded, but as a normal part of life's cycle and
the fulfillment of every individual's birthright.

I am most grateful to the many people who have given
help and advice during the writing of this text. In particular,
I would like to thank those who have most kindly given me
permission to use material from their own publications. These
include Age Concern for material from their discussion document 'Ageing in the 80s' by Bill Bowder and other documents published by them; Alison Norman for passages from
Rights and Risk published by the Centre for Policy on Ageing;
Doctor Alex Baker and the British Medical Journal for quotations from the paper 'Ageing and the Aged'; Alison Dunn,
Editor of the *Nursing Times* for material from 'The Elderly –
A Challenge to Nursing'; David Hobman, Anne Ebbett, Jane
Minter and Sally Greengross of Age Concern; John Wyatt
and Dorothy Mandelstam of the Disabled Living Foundation
and to the Beth Johnson Foundation and the World Health
Organization, Geneva for quotations from several of their
publications. I am deeply appreciative of the kindness and
generosity of all these individuals and organizations. Finally
I would like to thank Teresa de Bertodano of Darton, Longman & Todd for her great help in seeing this book through
the press.

Muriel Skeet
Geneva 1980

INTRODUCTION

Many of us will become old people. How do we view that prospect?

Probably many of us would answer that we dread the idea of getting old. Why? What does 'getting old' mean to us? Upon what do we base our expectations? What do we know about the ageing process?

Tragically, many people today often refer to old people as 'problems'. Rarely do they speak of them in terms of family or social solidarity. Only very infrequently are the positive contributions old people can make, to each other's lives as well as to those of other generations, recognized and acknowledged.

Because they make little or no contribution to the country's gross national product, old people have become so often, *unwanted* people. In all probability, therefore, we anticipate our own old age in terms of being unwanted, lonely, forgetful, confused and in the way. Yet many of these problems which are classified as being the results of age are no such thing.

Ageing is a *biological* process, determined, to a large extent, by our genes. Growing old, on the other hand, is a *social* process determined by our attitudes, expectations and the traditions of our society and culture. It is these latter which contribute to the preservation of myths which surround old age.

Let us first consider loneliness. There is no doubt that some old people are lonely. But there are lonely people of all ages. The worst thing about being lonely is being afraid of it.

Another common fear is not being wanted by family and friends. But that can happen to us at any age; throughout life we have to time our joining in with others and not expect a warm welcome when our family and friends are occupied with other things or other people.

Losing one's memory is one characteristic of ageing, which

most of us experience pretty early on in our lives. But to a certain extent one can arrest memory deterioration by training it. It helps *not* to write down everything. We can also avoid such absent-mindedness as not being able to remember whether we have cleaned our teeth by not 'absenting' our mind when we perform routine actions or habits. By concentrating on such tasks, alternating coloured toothbrushes for instance, we can strengthen memory. There are also those tricks we learnt at school when we needed to remember important facts or dates, and we can once again employ simple rhymes or acrostics to help us remember. Perhaps we deplore the fluttering indecision and lack of organization of some elderly people we know? Disciplining oneself *all* one's life to finish one job before beginning another can stand one in better stead.

Some men dread retirement and the fear of having nothing to do all day but 'getting in the way of the wife'. That certainly need not happen these days. Retirement can mean having time, but it also means having time to do things, learn things, visit places – and people. It can mean time for all those books one put off reading every weekend; to develop that interest or hobby one could never find enough time for; to improve one's game of golf or tennis or one's skill at crosswords or writing, painting or carpentry. And there are more opportunities for adult learning and education now than ever before.

Most voluntary organizations welcome new recruits to help with a wide range of activities, while there are several agencies up and down the country which specialize in jobs for the over-60s.

Love and sex? These too may change, but they need not disappear. As an eighty-year-old comments in John Masters' novel *The Field Marshal's Memoirs*, 'of course the love-making had not the frequency nor urgency of the old days, but because of that there was more beauty and infinitely more tenderness'.

And what of the spirit? John Masefield wrote:

> Man with his burning soul,
> Has but an hour of breath,
> To build a ship of Truth,
> In which his soul may Sail,

Sail on the sea of death,
For death takes toll of beauty, courage, youth,
Of all but Truth.

Our one 'hour of breath' can, as Masefield suggests, include putting the final touches to the 'ship of Truth'.

Certainly there is no need these days to see old age as Disraeli did, 'youth is a blunder; manhood a struggle; old Age a regret'. It is true that old age may probably contain regrets, but it need not consist totally of regretting. For old age is a part and a continuation of our lives, not a separate existence.

Yet, often, we try to make it so: we move house, change neighbourhoods and try to make new friends. Sometimes it may be society's expectations rather than our own personal circumstances which bring about such a move. In some instances, of course, it is a sensible action to take, but such a major decision requires careful consideration and a wide discussion of all alternatives.

In this country, we are fortunate in having many organizations and associations which provide information and assistance to help elderly people who are trying to reach such important decisions. Local Age Concern groups, for example, can give advice and the organization also produces many inexpensive or free informative booklets and pamphlets. The Citizens Advice Bureaux scattered throught the country will give advice on a number of subjects. Other organizations exist to help old people who have a disability or a specific need, while yet others, if requested, will provide help and advice relating to illness, dying or death.

This book, therefore, has four aims. First, it aims to help people to understand the ageing process; what it is, what it is doing to them and what it has done to others. Secondly, it is offered as a small contribution to help people to continue to enjoy being themselves and to reach personal fulfilment in their old age. The third aim is to provide information on the kind of practical help and services which are available to provide the necessary back up to self-help, family-help and community self-sufficiency. Its final aim is to enhance and enrich the lives of old people today, because readers will have acquired a better understanding of them.

For above all it is hoped that it will represent one small

step towards a better quality of life, not only for today's old people, but also for their children and grandchildren, indeed for ourselves.

PART I

THE AGEING PROCESS

Dum Loquimur, fugerit invida
Aetas, carpe diem, quam minimum credula postero.

While we're talking, time will have run meanly on:
Pick today's fruits, not relying on the future in the slightest.

Horace 65–68 B.C.

CHAPTER 1

OURSELVES AND THE PROCESS OF AGEING

Age I do abhor thee: youth I do adore thee.

The Passionate Pilgrim
William Shakespeare 1564–1616

All of us over the age of twenty are experiencing the process of ageing. Many generations and most cultures have fought the process, making use of a variety of substances ranging from ginseng to Guinness, oysters to Queen Bee Jelly, and employing a multitude of practitioners from beauticians to cosmetic surgeons. Since the time of Hippocrates (460–357 B.C.) at least 250 theories explaining the process have been put forward and an even larger number of ways for combating it have been suggested. To date, there is no known proven evidence that any substance or technique can slow down the process of ageing.

Longevity

All animals have an average life span. For human beings in industrialized countries it is now estimated to be approximately eighty years, the same as that of the whale. This, of course, is the *possible* life span: many people die before they reach such an age because disease or injury kills them prematurely. While it is believed that some genetic factors affect our rate of ageing and the length of our possible life span, we should not assume that we will die at the same age as our parents; habits and patterns of behaviour have a far greater effect than heredity.

Over the centuries, people have also sought ways to prolong life. Perhaps the best known literary example is that given in Aldous Huxley's blackest of black comedies *After Many a Summer*. It is the story of Jo Stoyte, a Californian millionaire with a pathological fear of death. Without doubt it is a moral fable for our time: the obsession with a quantity rather than

3

a quality of life. Incarcerating himself in a concrete castle and surrounded by armed guards Stoyte is like a mediaeval man living in daily dread of the plague and Dante's Inferno. With an eye to eternity he builds the Beverly Pantheon, a cemetery of monumental vulgarity complete with a pet's corner and a perpetual Wurlitzer. With an eye to longevity he keeps a luscious young mistress and the smooth and treacherous Doctor Obispo, whose job it is to prolong his master's life at whatever cost.

More recently, it has been advances in scientific knowledge and technology which have contributed to help the majority of us achieve our Third Age, although some of us are now questioning the quality of longevity when it means an artificially protracted existence. Perhaps it is harder for women than men to welcome the physical manifestations ageing brings. The looks of the latter often improve with age but the same cannot be said of most women. Few of us have that much admired 'ageless' bone structure and often we view with positive dislike the greying hair, sagging muscles, increasing girth and thinning skin. It is women, too, who face an acceleration of the ageing process in the form of those changes which take place at the time of the menopause.

Refusing to Grow Old

But while we cannot halt ageing, a normal biological process, we can refuse to grow old, which is a social process determined by attitudes, expectations and society's traditions. Ageing as a physical change is relatively unimportant compared with ageing as a social 'non-event'. We cannot change the fact that we are not immortal or indefinitely disease-proof or that certain illnesses may accumulate as we age. We can, however, do away with the social mythology of negative concepts of social ageing. We know, for instance, that the ability to retain new facts becomes poorer with age. This sometimes gives rise to the claim that part of the ageing process is a fall in the intelligence quotient (I.Q.). But the retention of new facts and other information is but one aspect of intelligence. Wisdom, that hybrid of a sense of proportion and judgement, actually increases and helps us to make much better use of the vast quantity of knowledge we have acquired. Wisdom is a scarce and valuable commodity. Very few young heads, apart from the one or two Portias around, are able to lay claim to it so we can put that important arrow in our quiver.

Arising from wisdom can come caution. Often in the past this has been mistaken for rigidity or 'mental arthritis'. Recent research however has suggested that it is not so much that old people *cannot* change but rather that they *will not* change, and usually for very good reasons. They see the risks involved and are content with the *status quo*, so they see no need to change. From the vantage point, in age, of our previous experiences and stored-up knowledge, we can better assess, balance and judge the change which is being proposed. What we must ensure, of course, is that we make an assessment and give a judgement after a thorough and open-minded examination of all possibilities and their effects, and that we are not swayed by either popular opinion, the vogue of the moment or a desire to be thought to be 'with it'.

Development During the Third Age

There is also evidence that our ability in other areas of intelligence, such as linguistic skill, continues to develop well into old age. This means that any field of education we undertake should be decided by taking into account those areas of learning in which we are most likely to excel. The method used for advanced education also merits consideration. We may require a different teaching approach from that used for younger people. Most of us received a very different education from that of today's young students and we should pay due regard to that fact when considering registering for any educational programmes.

The rewards of learning in youth are obvious: a better job, greater self-confidence, more authority and a higher salary. But education has its own absolute worth and does not have to be useful or undertaken in order to pass examinations or to compete in the rat race. Further education which develops interests and hobbies can certainly be looked forward to with pleasure.

The attitude towards knowledgeable old people is often ambivalent in our culture. It includes a tendency to assume that because someone is over a certain age, he or she must be out of touch and therefore cannot possibly know or understand. With increasing age, therefore, our views and opinions need to be clearly and concisely presented, and sometimes fairly forcibly, if we are not to be browbeaten. Otherwise, we ourselves can end up by believing that we have nothing to contribute. In order to form views and opinions we do, of course, need to equip ourselves with new knowledge and to keep up-to-date with the wealth of information which surrounds us. By so doing we can develop our own self-understanding further, as well as our sense of values. From that invaluable basis we can then contribute not only to the affairs of others, but also sensibly participate in deciding our own futures.

Social Life and Values

Our need to have an active, stimulating environment should also be borne in mind. We know that dynamic interaction among people of all ages and at all stages of development is vital to our well-being. Psychological experiments have shown that when young persons are exposed to reduced vision and hearing and lack of human contact, after only ten days the resulting monotony will cause them to show some of those effects which we associate with old age: apathy, loss of memory and mental confusion. It follows that the most effective way of preventing, postponing, or reducing the social and mental deterioration associated with (and sadly, often experienced in), old age is to ensure as full and active a setting as possible. Many of today's major problems of old age are in fact preventable because they exist either in the social or the economic field. Indeed, some of our present customs and cultures often *cause* problems. Compulsory retirement from gainful employment at a specified chronological age is just one example. Because of this, many of us from the age of sixty or sixty-five face economic deprivation, and some even poverty. When we are denied the right to be economically rewarded for the work we do, we are often denigrated as lacking the ability to carry out socially productive roles. This is related to a value which is central to present-day thinking: the equation of economic productivity with personal worth. There is, however, much evidence to show that not only are people of these ages able to work but they are also capable of learning different work and quite able to adjust to such a change.

An increasing number of elderly people experience loneliness. They lose, even in their family relationships, the feeling of being wanted or needed. Linked with all this is the tendency of the next generation to want to take over. Sometimes the old person is urged to 'rest and take it easy', or, in other words, to do nothing. Thus dependency can be created by the destruction of an individual's own capacities. This needs to be recognized and guarded against very early on in our preparation for old age.

Love and Sex

A full life includes love and expressions of love. Sexuality, the capacity to respond to another physically, need not decline as quickly nor so completely as fertility. The frequency of sexual intercourse is likely to decrease with age, either for psychological reasons or because of physical illness or disability. The main cause, however, is the widely held belief that sex is wrong, indecent or, at the very least, aesthetically undesirable for old people. Physical response to another during the Third Age often meets with strong disapproval and may even be called 'dirty'. Possibly this attitude developed because it was once believed that when her child-bearing age was past, a woman indulged in sexual intercourse only for carnal pleasure. These days, with a plethora of contraceptives available and an Abortion Act enforced, intercourse at every age takes place for enjoyment more often than for procreation. As we know from a recent survey undertaken by *The Observer*, many people in their seventies and beyond, need, and have, a sex life. Sadly, this is often kept secret. Yet as the sixty-year-old Field-Marshal's mistress says to her eighty-year-old lover in one of John Masters' novels, 'Everyone who reaches our age realizes that you don't feel any different inside yourself. You love just as much as you did twenty, thirty years before. It may look absurd from the outside but it doesn't seem so inside.'

Spiritual Development

Old age has always been thought of as a time for looking back over one's life: 'The unexamined life is not worth living,' wrote Socrates. This examination, of course, does not have to wait until we are old. Writing recently in *The Times*, Bernard

Levin commented: 'There are probably more people today
seeking some larger meaning or purpose in their lives and in
life in general than there have been, certainly in the West,
since the time of unquestioned faith.' He was reviewing Sir
Alistair Hardy's *The Spiritual Nature of Man* which bears a
considerable relationship to *The Varieties of Religious Experience*
published by William James in 1902. Sir Alistair's conclusion,
more cautious than that of James*, is well summarized in one
passage which Levin quoted in full: ' "The main characteristics of man's religious and spiritual experiences are shown
in his feelings for a transcendental reality which frequently
manifest themselves in early childhood: a feeling that the
'Something-other' than the self can actually be sensed; a
desire to personalize this presence into a deity and to have a
private 'I-Thou' relationship with it, communicating through
prayer." ' It is said that for many people this 'I-Thou' relationship is allowed to wither rather than develop during life.
Often it is only in old age that it is once more reconsidered
and desired. For some people the serenity and strength de-
rived from a religious belief elude them all their lives, even in
old age. Perhaps more attention is required to maintaining
spiritual 'youth' or at least the 'I-Thou' relationship of our
youth. To wait until the time of illness or approaching death
may mean waiting too long. One eminent British nurse who
has spent many years helping sick and dying people says of
today's old people, 'Most noticeable of all, is their sad lack
of inner resources with which to combat the bitterness of
loneliness and grief.'

Inner resources do not, of course, come overnight. The
contemporary Hungarian writer Gyula Illyes implies in *Ageing
in the Eighties* that people who have developed them are extremely rare. So rare, in fact, that he says, 'People who have
retained their spiritual youth in old age interest me much
more than the creatures of Mars if they ever came to Earth.'
Socrates gave his view to posterity thus: 'A man should feel
confident concerning his soul who has renounced those
pleasures and fineries that go with the body as being alien to
him and to consider them to result in more harm than in
good, but has pursued the pleasures that go with learning
and made the soul fire with no alien, but rather its own
refinements, moderation and justice and courage and freedom
and truth; thus is it ready for the world below.' It is easy to

see how far we, as creatures of the twentieth century are from that condition. For the majority of us, our bodily pleasures and fineries take priority instead of even a moderate place in our lives; we live in an age of excesses as well as deprivations and our world frequently denies justice and freedom and denigrates both physical and moral courage. It is little wonder therefore that we are not ready for any other world and cling to this one even when it means only a miserable existence. Is it perhaps because we are not ready for the inevitable end of old age that we refuse to prepare for its beginning?

We are, of course, the only living organisms who are bio-psycho-social beings and there is a close intertwining of these three elements in all phenomena of our individual as well as in our collective functioning. Many of the major questions concerned with ageing and related to the lives of old people touch on all three and answers therefore should be based on all three. Many difficulties resulting from socio-genic ageing for example, can, and must, be solved by communities them-selves using the welfare state merely for a support system or a back-up service. Even better, many difficulties can be pre-vented by the individual himself. As Plato said over two thousand years ago, 'Our discussion is no trifling matter but on the right way to conduct our lives.' Let us go on to consider some of them.

CHAPTER 2

UNDERSTANDING THE PROCESS AND SCIENCE OF AGEING

But an old age, serene and bright,
And lovely as a Lapland night,
Shall lead thee to thy grave.

'To a Young Lady'
William Wordsworth 1802

'The right way to conduct our lives' in our Third Age will be, inevitably, a personal, individual and varied decision. It should also be a considered decision, arrived at from relevant knowledge and from the selection of informed choices. In addition, it should be based upon some understanding of the process and the science of ageing.

This particular field of science is called gerontology. Gerontology is literally the science of ageing and relates to all and any aspects of it, ranging from the basic questions of what ageing is and what causes it, to such subjects as patterns of ageing in various cultures and historical periods. It also includes the planning of better services to meet the health and human welfare needs of older persons in various societies.

The content of gerontology evolves, therefore, from many scientific disciplines (biological, psychological and social), and it touches upon many professions, all of which attempt, to a greater or less degree, to alleviate those problems which are associated with ageing societies, groups and individuals. Primarily these are the human-cure and the human-care professions: medicine, nursing, various therapies and other health interventions, as well as social work, directly involved in the personal and social well-being of elderly people. Now that more of us are living to old age, other professionals are contributing to various aspects of gerontological theory and practice: architects, economists, sociologists, political scientists, lawyers, environmental planners, adult educationalists and so on.

As S. Tobin Sheldon has said, 'There is hardly any scientific field which is more universal than ageing, despite the variety of social and cultural settings in which humans live and age over time.' He continues, 'Gerontology as a scientific area affects the whole social structure. Gerontology has to be seen as a whole: in its foundation, its activities and its planning for the future.' It is this quality of universality which distinguishes ageing from disease.

Health really means 'wholeness'. It is a positive concept, meaning more than simply the absence of disease. It is not even just a normal functioning of cells, tissues and organs. While embracing all these, it is much more than their collectivity, because it involves a personal congruity with the individual's social environment. It is because many of us believe that health is not possible within a body affected by the changes of the ageing process that we often confuse old age with disease. But health and old age are not mutually exclusive. Old age does, however, have a number of qualities which it shares with disease: it is, for instance, intrinsic and its effects are cumulative.

There are, today, two major groups of theories about ageing. To use modern jargon, one group of theorists believe it is 'programmed' and the other that it is due to an accumulation of 'random errors'. The subject is well reviewed by Davies and Schofield, but briefly, the former believe that ageing is programmed in the same way as other stages of life: development in the womb (intra-uterine development), followed by body growth during the first twenty years, the reproductive period and the 'change' (menopause). Each of these stages marks 'a switching off' of the previous one and it is suggested by these theorists that once the full span has been achieved, life itself is 'switched off' by some mechanism residing in the genetic endowment of the organism (the individual person).

The second group hold theories which compare the ageing process with those of wear and tear. Their interest centres on the replication of D.N.A. (deoxyribonucleic acid in cells which carry inheritance), and the chance of random errors occuring which affect the energy and life of the cell, which, in turn, causes impairment of the organ (for example the heart) and ultimately of the organism (the individual person) itself.

There can be no doubt that errors of this type do occur

n ageing and, as an eminent British geriatrician J. Brock-lehurst, has stated, it is very likely that ageing is a multi-factorial process involving both groups of theories. To understand these and other current theories of ageing, for no one theory is universally accepted as yet, it is helpful to consider first the normal process of body maintenance.

Maintenance of the Human Body

All body tissue, bones, organs and muscles are composed of cells. Some of these cells are replaced continually. Blood cells, for instance, are renewed three times each year and skin cells also have a short life span. Some groups of cells have their own 'spare part' service. When specific types of tissue are destroyed by injury or infection, remaining cells take over the lost function either by becoming bigger or by reproducing replicas of those lost. But another type of cell, including those of the brain and nerves, can neither divide to produce replicas nor grow larger to take compensatory action. This explains one of the most common characteristics of the ageing process, the decreasing ability to remember.

Even in those groups which do reproduce copies of lost whole cells or their components, small errors sometimes occur and this can mean that function is never completely restored or that it takes a longer time to return. With ageing, therefore, cuts can take a longer time to heal and broken bones to unite.

The Ageing Body ~~∆s in oldage~~

Ageing also causes a diminution in the density of bone. This sometimes predisposes some compression of the bones which form the spinal cord (the vertebrae). Water is also lost from the discs of cartilage between the vertebrae. The result of these two processes is loss of height. Hence some old people appear to have 'shrunk'. The decrease in density means that bones become more brittle and break more easily. For this reason, a fall in old age often results in a broken bone.

Muscle cells exemplify the type which do not reproduce themselves, so consequently, with ageing, there is a decrease in their numbers. To a certain extent this can be compensated for if the size and power of the remaining ones are increased by exercise. This is one reason why regular physical exercise is important throughout the whole of one's life. Again, because of this decrease in muscle and lean body-mass and a corresponding increase in fat, a sensible well-balanced diet is vital in middle age if obesity is to be avoided.

Ageing also causes the skin to become thinner and transparent looking. Small blood vessels are therefore less well supported and rupture more easily. Even relatively minor knocks and injuries will cause severe bruising, while a fall can produce the transfer of a considerable amount of blood from the body circulation into those body tissues receiving the impact. This can cause a state of shock or collapse in the individual and is the reason why old people are more upset by and take longer to recover from an accident. It sometimes takes weeks or even months for the amount of blood to be made up or reabsorbed from the tissues back into the general circulation. Until this happens the injured person can feel very tired and even ill. Unless we understand this, the recovery period will not only be frustrating and depressing but the condition will also give rise to undue anxiety.

Changes due to ageing also affect fundamental body processes such as that of maintaining the upright position. This is, in fact, a highly complex feat which we developed late in our evolutionary scale. The upright body has a high centre of gravity, while the area of its base is relatively small. If the centre of gravity is not maintained over the base, the individual will fall. The upright posture is maintained by the contraction of opposing muscles but there is a constant tendency for the balance to be lost. This is appreciated immediately and subsconsciously through a sensory mechanism built into the skin, muscles, joints and even into the bones themselves. So, as soon as the centre of gravity alters, this is sensed and corrected by the opposing muscles. Posture is thus maintained against a background of sway. This sway can be seen in a toddler learning to walk or stand. Because of a slowing-down of nerve conduction and other aspects of neutronal function, the sway increases again in old age. It is for this reason that old people sometimes have difficulty in maintaining an upright position or are easily deflected from one. It also explains why, when they do stumble, they have great difficulty in saving themselves from a full-blown fall.

There are other important regulatory functions which are dependent upon the central nervous system and which are therefore impaired by the ageing process. The maintenance of body temperature is one; another is the maintence of blood pressure during changes of posture. This means that when old people get up quickly, perhaps to go to the lavatory in the middle of the night, they may become giddy and fall. This results from the gravitational pull which brings blood to the lower part of the body, thus depriving the brain of an adequate supply. It does not happen in younger people because of the immediate corrective reflexes throughout the central nervous system which increase the tone of the arteries in the lower part of the body, and thereby increase the heart's output. This corrective system is defective in old age.

Because of their position within the vertebrae, blood vessels supplying the bones of the spinal column are particularly prone to kinking as they pass up to the brain. When this happens, there can be momentary 'blackouts' or even neck and head discomfort of a longer duration.

Cells of the heart tissues may also be affected by age, as well as by disease. Changes in tissues of the chest wall and a decrease in the area of air sacs in the lungs (alveoli) can lead to the diminishing function of the heart and lungs. This accounts for the panting and breathlessness some people experience on exertion (for example when running after a bus). Once more, exercise can play a part in prevention. Even when exercise tolerance is small it may, with practice and training, be gradually increased.

The lymphatic system is also affected by ageing. This system operates through the white cells of the blood which normally attack and kill bacteria and viruses when they invade our bodies. These 'wars' take place in the lymph nodes and indications that they are being waged include swelling and pain. A common example is the small painful lumps which appear in the neck during the period of a sore (infected) throat. With ageing, not only do the replaced white cells prove to be less efficient, they may also attack other body tissues.

During the ageing process some of the physical changes can render an individual more susceptible to sensory deprivation, and these alterations may be augmented by pathological changes. For example, as the eye becomes older, some parts, particularly the lens and cornea, change slightly in shape. (Indeed, it is possible to estimate a person's age quite accurately with an ophthalmoscope as some of us who visit an optician for routine eye-testing are disconcerted to discover.) When this change occurs the ability to focus the image on the retina is reduced. If there is any indication that visual activity is changing arrangements for eye re-testing (or first-time testing) should be made. It is also important to ensure that new spectacles are comfortable, are kept clean and are worn. The cells of the retina also become less sensitive to light as one ages. On average, for satisfactory vision, people over eighty-five years of age need approximately eight times as much light as young people. This is why their rooms, stairs and steps should be very well illuminated.

The sense of hearing often becomes less acute as ageing progresses and a carefully prescribed hearing aid can make all the difference to the life of even a middle-aged person. If there is an impairment at such a comparatively early age, it is as well to recognize and accept it. It is far easier to use a hearing-aid when one can still discriminate and interpret varying sounds and pitches than to wait until a severe degree of deafness is experienced. At that stage some old people will need a good deal of encouragement to wear the aid as well as repeated, slow and patient instructions on how to use it. As neither hearing nor visual levels remain static, both should be checked regularly by specially trained people.

The sense of smell may diminish with age. While this can sometimes be an advantage, it can also take away some pleasures of life. It may also be a positive danger if, for example, escaping gas is not noticed.

Taste may be affected and for gourmets and wine-lovers this is a particularly sad loss. Many people find that they require more seasoning with their food, though an excess of salt with meals is not recommended especially if one's blood pressure is high or there is fluid retention from any disease. Some people even develop a new liking for spicy Oriental foods.

Our sense of touch is lost only through disease, as for example, when diabetes affects the nerve endings or a stroke results in an inability to move part of one's body. In the latter instance, the affected side of the body will also be insensitive to touch. The obvious dangers of this will need to be recognized and guarded against.

In all body systems, the functional effect of ageing is more apparent when the body is stressed than when it is at rest. This applies in instances which range from the ability of the digestive system to deal with a high intake of sugar, to the ability of the kidneys to maintain their power to excrete urine. Changes in the glandular (endocrine) system are also more apparent under stress and demands made upon endocrine glands will affect their activities. The thyroid gland in the neck for example, which controls metabolism, is likely to have less demands made upon it as the bodily activity lessens. The decline of sex hormones in women is most apparent at the time of the menopause: oestrogen declines much less after the age of sixty than between the ages of forty and sixty. The male sex hormone gradually diminishes from the time of maturity. But the end of the fertility period does not mean the end of sexuality.

These are some of the basic changes of ageing which *may* affect physical health. The overall effect of the process is an increasing fraility of the body with a slowing-down of its functions. None is disastrous: most are merely inconvenient and all can be experienced without the individual's health being affected whatsoever.

The Ageing Mind

The cells of the central nervous system (neurones) are another group of cells which do not reproduce themselves. During ageing their function is gradually impaired and their number may also decrease. The effect of this is probably most apparent in memory, particularly in committing new matter to memory. It becomes easier to remember the long-ago past rather than the immediate past. This explains why some old people are often said to 'live in the past', as they repeat stories of their younger days time and time again.

With age, thinking can also become more rigid and fixed and the acceptance of new ideas or the absorption of new information may become progressively more difficult. But that diffficulty can be experienced by a 'mentally arthritic' forty-year-old, while some old people are flexible in their thinking and bubbling over with new ideas on their eightieth or even ninetieth birthdays.

Intellectual deterioration is often considered to be a result of ageing. In fact, our intellectual abilities decline from about sixteen or seventeen onwards. We can, of course, gain new experiences and knowledge and these compensate for that deterioration. This is another reason why an alert mind 'exercising' itself with the exploration of new ideas, opinions, situations, outlooks and doctrines, will keep itself flexible and in 'good shape'. To deny such opportunities to an old person will obviously have the opposite effect. Dis-use atrophy is a very real thing. Just as an unused muscle wastes, so does an unused mind. This is why it is important to encourage old people to think for themselves and to participate in decision-making and planning, particularly that which concerns their own lives. Gross deterioration in memory, loss of emotional control and diminished ability to reason can all happen, but they only happen to a small minority. The fact that they sometimes happen does not prove that they are direct results of ageing. Often these losses are caused by monotonous daily régimes consisting of mere physical existence.

Another misheld belief concerns dementia. Old age does not bring dementia. It is a disease affecting a minority of old people, just as, for example, multiple sclerosis is a disease affecting a minority of young people.

What of personality? What of the cantankerous old woman or the irascible old Colonel? As Tony Whitehead maintains, there is considerable truth in the statement, 'If you want to be a charming old lady, you have first to be a charming young lady!' (This applies to gentlemen too.) Personality traits, both those which are acceptable and those which are not, do not disappear or change with ageing, they simply intensify. The kind, well-mannered young man becomes the thoughtful courteous old man, while the bad-tempered youth becomes the paranoid, irritable old boy.

Ageing and the Emotions

Emotional conflicts, inhibitions and other emotional maladjustments can occur at any age. Only those people who are indifferent to others live a life free from all tensions. When we are very active, however, such difficulties are often pushed into the background and may not have an effect on our behaviour, but with retirement, family relationships become even more important. If for example, a marital relationship has never been good and problems have not been worked through at an earlier stage, they will be dramatically intensified when the couple are thrown together day in and day out. The emotional repercussions at this time can be great. But they are also preventable, for the problem could have been dealt with years before. Of course, family problems rarely occur in isolation: often they are an interwoven complex of emotion, body functioning (or malfunctioning), and interactions with people and societies. Sometimes outside help can produce a solution or at least a better quality of life. That 'multidisciplinary' team of our Welfare State can often be called upon to good effect in terms of the old person being helped to help himself or his or her supporter supported.

It is perhaps in the spiritual field that ageing can bring optimism and joy. Mental, physical and emotional processes may change, atrophy or diminish, but spiritual 'ageing' can mean spiritual development and growth. But now, let us go on to consider the kind of future background against which all this is likely to happen, for this will affect all our lives.

CHAPTER 3

A BRIEF SOCIAL AND ECONOMIC BACKGROUND TO AGEING IN THE EIGHTIES

One of the major factors relating to providing care facilities for elderly people is the increase in the proportionate populations of those over sixty-five and seventy-five years. 'Population Projections 1976–2016', published by the Office of Population Censuses and Surveys, showed the following predictions of the increasing population in the UK:

an increase of 3.5 per cent in the total number of people over retirement age;

an increase of 21.3 per cent in the number of people over 75 years;

an increase of 40 per cent in the number of people over 85 years.

> *Ageing in the Eighties*, a discussion document for the 1980 Age Concern Study Conference.

William Blake wrote, 'As a man sees, so he is.' The way we 'see' the world influences what we become, what we make of ourselves, how we live in our own company and the company of others and how we behave towards ourselves and other people. So our vision of what it is to be old influences what we make of our own old age. And judging by projected statistics, the majority of us will live to old age. What major influences are and will be at work in our lives?

The Influence of Literature

Human beings, Stella Claydon has suggested in *Images of Age*, appear to need to make 'stories' out of their lives or those of others. As far as their own lives are concerned they need to see the 'stories' as continuing paths reaching some kind of conclusion, 'whether it be mountain top or home-coming'. The final arc of one's life is one in which we are likely to do a great deal of retrospection, turning over past experiences in order to find some thread of meaning running through them, the present and the future. Failure to find meaning results in feelings of frustration and hopelessness. Success in finding meaning on the other hand, results in a sense of fulfillment and that traditional wisdom of old age, the quintessence of a lifetime's experience. This explains to some extent the contentment of some old people and the despair of others.

Maslow speaks in *Motivation and Personality* of the need of man, 'to discover the final stage of his life', and 'to move towards the guiding image, the unfulfilled promise'. 'It is', he writes, 'when old age is perceived as a stage at which no guiding image is seen, that despair and a feeling of the emptiness of life come.' It is important for those who have contact with old people to understand and appreciate this point. In *Endgame*, Beckett gives a vision of the end of life (of *all* life we are led to imagine) full of meaningless suffering, where day succeeds meaningless day, 'grain upon grain, one by one, and one day, suddenly, there's a heap, a little heap, an *impossible* heap.' Blind, bored, unable to move and horribly sadistic, the old man Hamm torments his servant Clov while, even more terribly deprived and immobile, his aged parents live out the remainder of their existence in significantly symbolic dustbins.

But perhaps life which has no meaning is best symbolically represented by, 'Sans teeth, sans eyes, sans taste, sans everything'. Shakespeare put these words into the mouth of his cynic Jacques, in *As You Like It*, who saw all stages of life as ugly and ridiculous and all equally without meaning. But Shakespeare goes on to give the alternative vision of human life and old age: immediately after Jacques has spoken, a real old man enters. He represents kindliness, heroic duty and love. His very name, Adam, indicates that he represents humanity. He is helped in by the young man Orlando, whose life he has saved and who, in turn, is now protecting him.

The loss of a sense of the *cycle* of life is, perhaps, part of the divided self of man living in our modern industrialized society. Rejection of old age as a stage of life during which growth and change may take place impoverishes our view of human life as a whole. Erikson also makes this point in *Insight and Responsibility*. 'Western psychology has avoided looking at the range of the whole cycle . . . of individual life coming to a conclusion. . . . Any span of life lived without vigorous mean-

ing –whether at the beginning, in the middle or at the end –
endangers the sense of life and the meaning of death.'

Symbolic images of age have been presented by myth and
dream: in them, old age is seen as representing certain qualities and values necessary to the whole human being. They
are apprehended in an external figure to which Jung has
given the name, 'the wise old man'. This is the figure which
appears in dreams as a priest, doctor, teacher or grandfather
and appears in mythology and fairy stories as a seer or magician. Figures such as Merlin, the blind seer Teiresius and
Gandalf, the magician in *The Lord of the Rings*, are but a few
examples. In literature we also have the Ancient Mariner,
King Lear and Oedipus at Colonus. Jung, in *Four Archetypes*,
comments that the figure of the wise old man appears in
situations in which the dreamer (or the hero of fairy tale or
mythology), cannot find resources in himself to solve his problems, although, in fact, he possesses them. In the figure of a
wise old man, he finds an external image of a strength which
seems to be outside himself. He therefore appears in a situation, 'where insight, understanding, good advice, planning
etc. are needed but cannot be mustered on one's own resources'. He adds, 'the old man . . . represents knowledge, reflec-
tion, insight, wisdom, cleverness and intuition on one hand
and moral qualities such as goodwill and readiness to help
on the other.'

But not all real old people are wise. Is this why, in our
disappointment, we often become impatient and frustrated
with them or why, sometimes, we reject them and organize
their removal from our sight?

We also learn from literature, however, that old age *can* be
a stage of growth, of learning and of development of the self.
How can we make it so, against the projected socio-economic
background of the '80s? Let us now consider some likely
developments.

Effects of Employment and Retirement.

The imposition of compulsory retirement is an artifact of our
modern industrial society. There is not, nor has there ever
been, anything special about the age of sixty or sixty-five,
when a woman or a man must cease to undertake paid work.
These ages are a product of actuarial calculation, based on

the length of time the government might reasonably be sup-
posed to have to pay out a pension before a man or woman
dies, the demands of the political need to maintain nearly full
employment and the need to provide, within some organizations, movement up a hierarchy of responsibility and remu-
neration. Compulsory retirement can be and is used as a way
of getting rid of people who are either no longer needed or no
longer approved of by their employers. More positively, it is
also seen as a reward for those who have worked in strenuous
manual labour all their lives.

Mandatory retirement and its link with pensions has had
a singularly disastrous effect on the way society thinks of
those either approaching or beyond retirement age. The ages
of sixty or sixty-five are increasingly seen as watersheds.
Chronological ages, plucked out of the air are, for a large
section of society, a time when they cease to have anything
but a token significance. They are suddenly removed from
positions where they may have been required to perform
intricate or dangerous industrial tasks, or be responsible for
lives, large sums of moneys or the development of large commercial concerns, and expected to be content to just grow
roses or read the daily newspaper. There is often a desperate
attempt made by such people to assure everyone that, 'I am
busier now than before I retired', thereby trying to maintain
the right to be regarded as a part of the essential and needed
working populace. Nevertheless, their 'busyness' emphasizes
the fact supported by the findings of various studies that they
are quite capable of work. Many of these studies have indicated that in terms of reliability, time-keeping and aptitude
for their jobs, older workers perform as well, if not better,
than their younger colleagues.

The rapidity with which jobs become outdated and new
skills have to be learnt is increasing. Probably the need to be
retrained a number of times during one's working life will
become common. Inevitably there will be many who cannot,
or will not, be retrained, but these may not necessarily be
older people. Redundancy is hitting both young and old, and
the resulting disruption in the natural evolution of our working lives may reduce the emphasis placed on compulsory
retirement. Because there is little evidence that the older
worker is less able to pick up new skills than the younger,
aptitude and ability, not age, could well become the signifi-

cant criteria for whether one is employed or not. Further, with the large increase in overall unemployment in this country (some predict about six million by the mid-'80s), the statutory retirement age will not be such a harsh dividing line as it is at present, because many people may have been out of work for the greater period of their 'working' lives or may, at least, have experienced a two or three-day week for the latter part of them.

Problems of the unemployed, both young and old, could be tackled together. It is not age, but income, status and a sense of purpose which are likely to be the problems of the future. (Unfortunately we are already seeing the effects an absence of these are having on some of our young people.) To some degree, those of us who are experiencing old age at the present time share the lot of these other non-productive sectors of our population. At retirement age we are cut off abruptly from paid employment. We find ourselves reduced to the status of a dependant and, more than likely, of a recipient. This sudden break from occupational activity can be frequently accompanied by a steady deterioration in health. Some people believe that no mandatory retirement age should exist, but rather, we should all have the right of choice. Certainly, the present arrangement has disadvantages, as the rate of biological ageing varies significantly from one individual to another.

Effects of the Fuel Crisis
Havighurst, of Chicago University, predicts a higher retirement age for Western society because of the world's fuel crisis. He predicts that after 1990, the economic structure of the developed societies will be dominated by the supply and the cost of energy. Until now, the twentieth-century industrialization of the 'affluent third' of the world's people has been based essentially on cheap petroleum, steel, aluminium, lumber, papers, plastics and fertilizers. These are becoming increasingly scarce and expensive. If the present rate of use continues, by the year 2,000, just one generation away, the world's supply of petroleum and natural gas will be nearly used up. Coal will be available for at least another fifty years but, in human labour per unit of energy, will cost more than petroleum. The most generally accepted prediction for West-

ern Europe and North America is that the cost of a unit of
energy in the year 2,000 will be at least four times what it
was in 1980.

Havighurst suggests that, assuming the continuation of a
democratic political structure moving towards a somewhat
greater government participation in the economy (already
happening in the UK) and also assuming that we shall have
no major war, there are two contrasting futures tolerable for
a population which has achieved a zero population growth
rate and which has to come to terms with the need to maintain
an equilibrium between the use of energy and other critical
materials and their creation or restoration. The proper use of
human resources and the education and development of human beings will be essential for both alternatives. In other
words, the success of our society will depend upon the efficiency with which energy, capital and labour are used.

A major increase in costs of energy, together with certain
scarce critical materials, argues Havighurst, will tend to lower
the material standard of living in our industrialized countries.
People will probably respond by working more years or more
hours, in order to increase the production of goods and services and thereby maintain a standard as close to their present
one as possible. Elderly people, therefore, will be encouraged
to stay in the labour force as long as they remain reasonably
productive. One may even imagine, he writes, that 'the notion
of mandatory retirement at a fixed age will be forgotten, and
the average age for voluntary retirement will be about seventy. There may also be considerable development of part-
time employment, an ideal arrangement for older workers.'
This could mean more emphasis on research with the aim of
fitting work-assignments to people with the knowledge, skills
and strength appropriate to the tasks to be undertaken. The
work of Leon Koyl in this field – matching persons over the
age of fifty with jobs to be done – could be given impetus.
The work of Belbin in the retraining of older workers for new
jobs, might also be more favourably considered in this
country.

All this, of course, paints a very different picture from that
of the immediate past, our present and also the short-term
predictions which are being made. The latter are also worth
looking at as, in practical terms, they will affect our own old
age.

Effects of Transport Developments

During the '60s and '70s with abundant and comparatively inexpensive energy, it became an established pattern for children to move away from their parents to live and work, and return to visit them at weekends or Bank Holiday times. In the near future such visits may well become fewer, because of their prohibitive cost. As grandparents, therefore, we may see less of our families than we do as parents. Public transport, particularly buses, coaches and taxes will also be affected by the high cost of fuel. The train service in this country, because of recent reductions in track and the difficulty of getting porters to handle luggage has not been an ideal form of travel for old people for some years, though many thousands of elderly people frequently make use of British Rail concessions.

Effects of Communication Development

Ironically, the communication explosion is not likely to increase direct contact with others. Not only are telephone costs prohibitive, but the future may mean fewer face-to-face meetings. The processing of information on financial matters, social security benefits and travel facilities by silicon chip will mean that we will not need to actually *visit* our bank manager, tax inspector, post-mistress, solicitor or travel agent. The owner of a telephone and a television set will be able to obtain, through the development of central computer systems like Ceefax (The BBC's information service), and Prestel (the Post Office's information system), virtually any information he or she wants, without speaking to anyone. While this may increase the efficiency of those organizations which are, at present, in direct communication with the public, it will sever many lines of personal contact for, among others, elderly people who are already somewhat isolated through not working or not living near their families. It will mean that more effort to go out and about will need to be made.

Effects of New Shopping Methods

In the same way that the development of supermarkets has caused the near elimination of local small shops in our towns and cities, this kind of automation may soon cease to be an option. It may well become the *only* way of getting day-to-day information. We already have a foretaste of what this will mean in the processing of our gas and electricity bills. The automation of shopping and accounting procedures will penalize those who prefer traditional ways of shopping, because the latter will be more expensive. The computerized direct debits of customers' accounts will eliminate cash handling and this saving by supermarkets together with the high cost of haulage, will be reflected in comparative prices. Conversations with shopkeepers and personal contacts with their assistants will disappear.

Effects of More Leisure Time

Sometimes it is not easy to distinguish leisure activities from work. Sitting on local Councils, organizing a jumble sale or coffee morning, or arranging flowers for the local church – are these work or leisure activities? Such a question touches at the root of our attitudes towards the unemployed, towards work and towards old people. It is a question which will become increasingly insistent as the micro-chip revolution and the no-growth economy force more people out of work at an earlier age. What people do when they are not in full-time paid employment is linked to who they are and who they believe themselves to be. Leisure is related to our image of ourselves. As leisure begins to dominate life, either because of increasing unemployment or because of enforced retirement from paid employment, the question will become increasingly important and increasingly inescapable – who are we?

It is possible that with a general increase in society's leisure time, the distinction between the old as a leisured class (but often with limited money with which to enjoy their leisure) and the rest of the population, will be reduced. As leisure activities become throughout life an increasingly important part of the business of living, old people should have more and better opportunities for continuing and joining with others of different ages. The artificial creation of 'things to do' in old age will then be rejected in favour of developing life-long interests.

Effect of More Learning Opportunities

The idea that old dogs cannot learn new tricks has too often, and inappropriately, been applied to old people. The fact is that old people can and do learn very well, given the right conditions and suitable teaching methods. Perhaps one of the most important developments in this field in recent years has been the establishment by Royal Charter in 1969 of the Open University. Like other British universities, the Open University is empowered to grant its own degrees. It is also charged with a responsibility to further the educational well-being of the community as a whole. The BBC provides a wide range of courses combining radio and television with written publications. An increasing number of universities, polytechnics and colleges of higher education are running courses in higher education especially for adults, while a wide range of subjects is offered in courses organized by correspondence colleges.

Accumulated wisdom has always been invaluable. Now old people have the opportunity as never before to equip themselves with *new* knowledge. The resulting combination offers a unique and important role in the development of our society.

Effects of the Religious Revival

There are signs that the spiritual needs of both the old and of children are being taken increasingly seriously after a period in which anything spiritual was regarded as little better than superstitious nonsense, which, if left to itself, would wither away. Religion, for the past decade or so, has been regarded by opinion formers, the media, many educationalists and social scientists, as a prop and support for weak minds, be they minds in their first or second childhood. At best, religious experience has been treated as an optional extra like music or fencing at schools – fine if you like that sort of thing, but not essential to the curriculum of life.

Two things seem to be effecting a change in this attitude. The first is the increasing amount of research into religious experience, and the second is the greater awareness of the deep-rooted nature of religious feeling throughout the world. Religion is *not* withering away. This has become all too apparent to observers of the Islamic revival in the Middle East and the Christian response to the Pope's international tours. In this country, television, which had kept religion in a 'Godslot' on Sundays, has begun to feature religious programmes at prime viewing times and it is reported that programme controllers have not been disappointed by viewing figures.

But the emphasis which many religions tend to place on corporateness can itself clash with the increasing sense of individuality of an old person. As Christianity, for example, seeks new forms of worship to underline its corporateness, some old people feel alienated from public worship, a tendency which is exacerbated by increasing physical difficulties of getting to church. Studies undertaken in the USA suggest that while the sense of spiritual needs increases as one gets older, the wish to participate in corporate religious practice decreases. This has clear implications for religious organizations which see their main task as assembling the communal 'family' for worship each week.

Effects of Current Information Revolution

Writing for Age Concern, Bill Bowder, an experienced journalist in the social services, also sees the current information revolution as holding a threat to the individual. He believes that: 'The tendency of the statistical approach to people's needs,expectations and habits, to erect a norm of behaviour, can then be used to question and down-grade the individual responses of people who do not feel that they are having their needs, expectations or patterns of life met.' He goes on to say:

This process is not new – the continual collection of data about virtually every aspect of the behaviour of a population has been going on for years, as has the refusal to accept the validity of people's experiences when they run counter to the mass behaviour described by researchers. But the continued explosion of information collection and collation threatens to promote the 'ironing out' effect at an increased rate. Not only will shopping and living patterns be increasingly dictated by such generalised 'consumer research', but also will psychological behaviour and biological patterns be increasingly judged against norms which will brook little opposition. The eccentric, the individual, the crotchety, the moody, the misfit will not only not be catered for, he or she will come increasingly under pressure commercially, socially and medically to fit in with the norms . . . not only will the individual be seen as odd, he will be seen as bad. The general social trend will, then, be towards greater personal isolation coupled with greater pressure to conform by buying, feeling, thinking, doing as everyone else does.

Whether Bowder is right or not, it is obviously wise not only to try to understand and accept old age, but also to prepare and plan for it individually. In Part II we will consider ways in which we can prepare and plan to maintain independence for as long as possible.

PART II

MAINTAINING INDEPENDENCE

The first of earthly blessings, independence.

Autobiography
Edward Gibbon 1737–1794

CHAPTER 4

DECIDING WHERE TO LIVE

Mid pleasures and palaces though we may roam,
Be it ever so humble, there's no place like home;
A charm from the skies seems to hallow us there,
Which, seek through the world, is ne'er met with elsewhere.
Home, home, sweet, sweet, home!
There's no place like home! There's no place like home.

'Clari, The Maid of Milan'
J. H. Payne 1823

One of the first and most important decisions to make for ourselves or with elderly people for whom we have some responsibility, is where to live, and may sometimes include with whom to live.

If each one of us were asked how we would like our old age to be, the majority would answer that we hope to remain in our own homes, in control of our faculties and to lead a happy, useful life, with full independence. While there might be differences of opinion regarding what makes life 'happy', 'useful', and even 'independent', for the most part there is likely to be agreement on the hope that we would be in full control of our lives, lived out in our own homes. The vast majority of people who are facing old age today would probably give a similar reply. How can they achieve it and how can we achieve it against the backgrounds of economic, social and physiological changes we have discussed?

Prevention of those diseases which are associated with old age is one obvious answer. A sensible way of living throughout the whole of one's life certainly helps: moderation in things such as food and alcohol; abstention from other potentially lethal addictives such as cigarette nicotine and drugs, and an awareness and commitment to the more positive steps which can be taken. These include adequate exercise, sufficient work and learning, adequate relaxation, being in the company of other people, having interesting hobbies and recreational activities and taking a diet which is well balanced in both quality and quantity.

First, we need to alter our thinking that old age inevitably represents a problem. Many people enjoy an active, happy and contented old age. A large number of people accomplish the whole process of ageing with little or no recourse to health professionals, psychiatrists or social services. Nothing terrible suddenly happens to a man or woman on their sixtieth or sixty-fifth birthday. Yet we have almost decreed that when they reach that milestone, they can no longer manage their own lives. Furthermore, by growing up with that kind of idea in our minds, we are far more likely to approach those birthdays in our own lives with mounting dread and some of us even begin to act according to our preconceived ideas. Others, thank goodness, refuse to be bullied into that state. A few months ago, a sixty-year-old woman wrote to the editor of a Sunday newspaper, saying:

> Pensioners are being got at. We must prepare to do battle to maintain our independence and to preserve our attractive personalities. I am haunted by the fear that if I cannot dispel the assumption that I am 'a senior citizen', the following events will occur:
>> I shall have a gang of young thugs sent to my home to paint my kitchen (instead of their being sent to prison);
>> I shall have patients from the local mental hospital drafted to dig my garden;
>> I may be forced to go to 'suitable entertainment' to drink tea;
>> I shall be expected to attend a party and wear a paper hat at Christmas;
>> I may receive vast boxes of assorted food to which I feel I am not entitled . . .
>
> We pensioners are in a terrifying position – we have been forced to become recipients . . . Hands off please . . . I am in charge of my life.

That opening paragraph makes an interesting point, 'We must prepare to do battle to . . . preserve our attractive personalities.' She implies that we can almost *cause* older people to become less attractive personalities. Certainly several researchers have reported that old people are likely, in time, to accept whatever role is attributed to them. So those attitudes of many of us, expecting an old age pensioner to be sick, 'ga-ga' or a nuisance need to undergo fundamental change. An old person's home is still his castle; he is still the host in it, and he can be helped to remain so.

Census figures of 1971 showed that 94 per cent of all persons over that inspired age of sixty-five years lived in private households. Fifty per cent of these were owner-occupiers, about 34 per cent housing association or local authority tenants and the remainder private tenants. A high level (87 per cent) of those sampled in the privately-housed group expressed satisfaction with their accommodation and this finding, by Age Concern (1974) was consistent with the General Household Survey of a few years before. That had shown that only 10 per cent of elderly people were seriously considering or wanting to move house.

Reasons for dissatisfaction among the unhappy group were related to social and physical difficulties associated with the accommodation itself; poor facilities, such as an outside w.c.; the size of accommodation too large to keep clean; poor access to it with too many steps or stairs, and dissatisfaction with the neighbourhood or neighbours due to changes in the local population. It is obvious that with such a variation in reasons there can be no one solution from the government or anyone else, which will affect happiness or even give satisfaction for all. But equally, no obstacle presented was insurmountable, each required personal assessment, discussion, planning and action with the old person concerned. Laws, Acts, bountiful handouts of state largesse were not the answer; family, friends, neighbours and the surrounding community often are.

Local authorities had, and still have, a range of powers to assist elderly people with housing. Of particular importance are those concerned with structural grants. 'Housing Policy: A Consultative Document', was published in 1977 by the government of that time. It suggested that repair and maintenance should be supported rather than improvement of housing. Adaptations referred to in the publication include ramps, bath aids, kitchen aids and heating assistance as well as telephones and alarm systems.

While all this sounds splendid in documents, even before recent governmental financial cut-backs it was very difficult to obtain all the necessary help through these channels.

Knowledge of what is available, who is eligible and how to apply are only part of the problem. Many people assess their home in the light of, at best, increasing frailty. Decisions regarding any action will, of course, be influenced by financial resources and by any alternative accommodation which is available.

Owner-occupiers may decide either to have improvements or adaptations made to their home, or to sell and move to a smaller and more easily-run house. People who live in rented accommodation may also consider the possibility of having adaptations carried out or renting a more suitable flat or house. Others may consider having a tenant themselves, moving to friends or relations or to sheltered accommodation, an almshouse or a nursing home. So how does one decide? First, it should be said that moving home should never be undertaken lightly and all possibilities should be discussed before such a major decision is made. While the following information is by no means exhaustive, it may provide a starting point.

Owner-occupiers

a) Making Improvements or Repairs to One's Own Home

If owner-occupiers decide that they can and should remain in their present home, providing some adaptations are possible, they can apply for a house renovation grant. Three types are available: improvement grants, intermediate grants and repairs grants.

To apply for any one of these, it is necessary to call or write to the nearest City Engineer's Department or to the Chief Environmental Health Officer's Department. An Improvement Grant Officer of the former, or a Housing Officer of the latter will arrange for one of his staff to visit and discuss the proposed plan. After a plan has been agreed upon and an estimate made, a formal application for the grant can then be made to the local Council. If the Council decides to make the requested grant, it will send an inspector to determine 'the eligible expense' of the proposed work. At that point, evidence will have to be submitted to the city solicitor proving the occupier's legal title to the property.

General Conditions Attached to All Grants Are:

    the dwelling must not have been built before October 2nd 1961 (before 1919 for a repair grant);

    the applicant must be a freeholder or have a lease with at least five years to run;

    the dwelling must be used in the manner described on the applicant's certificate for a period of at least five years;

    application for the grant must be made before the work is undertaken. This application must include: (i) a plan, in duplicate, illustrating the dwelling before and after the proposed improvement has been made; (ii) an estimate of the cost of the proposed work; (iii) a certificate of future occupation, in duplicate.

Improvement Grants

These grants are those made by a Council either to improve or repair older houses to a higher standard or convert large houses into flats. They are discretionary.

In addition to the general conditions listed above, there are specific conditions related to this type of grant. Usually such a grant is not awarded if the property is to be occupied by the owner and its rateable value exceeds £225 (£400 in Greater London), *or* if the building is to be converted into flats, the owner intends to occupy one of them and the rateable value exceeds £350 (£600 in Greater London).These limits do not apply for dwellings in housing action areas or where the grant is for work to improve a home for a disabled person. Although in some cases the local council may reduce the standards, normally:

    the property should have a minimum life of thirty years;

    all standard amenities should be in a good state of repair after the proposed improvements have been made;

    not more than 50 per cent of the total expense can be attributed to repair work. If homes are in need of substantial structural repair this may be increased to 70 per cent.

The maximum cost for which a grant may be aided is £5,500 for non-priority cases and £8,500 for priority cases (i.e. houses in housing action areas or houses in particularly bad conditions – e.g. unfit for habitation, lacking standard amenities or in need of substantial structural repair). This rises to £7,500 and £11,500 respectively in Greater London. The 'priority rate' of grant is now available for improvements for disabled people.

If the property owner is unable to contribute the remainder, the possibility of receiving a maturity loan should be discussed with the Housing Advice Centre staff or the local housing authority. Improvement grants are also available for work to adapt a house for a disabled person.

Intermediate Grants

These grants are available as of right to help meet the cost of installing standard amenities for the first time (hot and cold water supply for bath and shower, wash-basin, kitchen sink and w.c.) They can cover certain repair or replacement work if it is carried out at the same time. (It is not necessary for standard amenities to be installed at the same time in order to obtain a grant).

Normally, in addition to the general conditions, one specific conditions relating to this type of grant is that once the work is completed the house or flat should be 'fit for human habitation'. But if it feels it is reasonable to do so, the council can waive this condition.

Intermediate grants are also available to provide extra standard amenities if existing ones cannot be reached by a disabled occupant.

Repair Grants

Repair grants are available only for houses or flats built before 1919. To qualify for a repairs grant (which is discretionary), the work must be substantial and structural and the council must be satisfied that, after the work is done, the dwelling will be in reasonable repair. The rateable value of the home must be under £225 (£400 in Greater London). These limits do not apply to dwellings in housing action areas.

Householders should never initiate improvements or repairs in the hope that this will strengthen their applications. It will *not* do so.

b) Having Adaptations Made to One's Own Home

If the onset of a disability renders a home very inconvenient or impossible to live in, assistance for adaptations may be given through an improvement grant. Typical adaptations include the building of a ramp for a wheelchair at the approach to the home; the installation of a downstairs bathroom and w.c.; the conversion of a bathroom to a shower room; the installation of a chair-lift. Social services departments can also help with the provision of other special facilities for disabled people.

c) Selling One's Home

Selling one's own home is a very big step to take. It is one which is often bitterly regretted later on, especially if the decision has been made immediately after bereavement. There is a temptation when a spouse dies for the husband and, more especially the wife, to up-sticks and try to begin a new chapter. Laudable though this may appear in some respects, it is wise to wait a year before coming to such a major decision. Some elderly people, on the other hand, stay on in a large hard-to-run house which is totally unsuitable for their new needs, purely for sentimental reasons. While this is perfectly understandable, the pros and cons of living under such circumstances should be carefully thought out, bearing in mind the possibility of increasing dependency upon others.

Moving house at any age, of course, has considerable disadvantages: one moves from friends and neighbours, from known tradespeople and from a general practitioner who, sadly less often now than in the past, knows one's family and medical history. Furniture and other valued possessions may have to be sold, and above all there is the difficulty of adapting to a new environment. Some people lessen the loss by moving to a smaller house but within the same neighbourhood, but this of course is not always possible.

Whether one intends to buy another home or not, it is desirable to sell before moving. If another purchase is intended, a bridging loan may be arranged with the bank manager, but like all loans at the present time, this will prove very expensive. If it is not intended to buy another property, the local authority can be approached. Some buy a home in return for rehousing the owner. The director of the local housing authority should be asked whether he would be interested in buying. Full details of the house including its current state of repair should be given in writing.

Some housing associations will also buy homes of elderly people, convert them into several flatlets and make one of them available to the previous owner. This does mean, of course, that short-term accommodation must be found whilst the conversion work is being carried out.

Buying a New Home

Before contacting an estate agent to find a new home, one's essential requirements should be identified and listed. Estate agents are listed in telephone directories or a list of members of the National Association of Estate Agents may be obtained from Arbon House, 21 Jury Street, Warwick.

Those who wish to buy a property in an area of the country other than that in which they are living can write to National Homes Network. This is a national network of estate agents which exists for this purpose. It gives information free of charge. Enquiries should be addressed to them at Suite 303, Radnor House, 93 Regent Street, London W1.

When suitable property has been successfully located, an offer to buy 'subject to contract' should be made through a solicitor. A surveyor should be appointed, not only by the lending organization but also by the individual purchaser. Each will be looking at different aspects and conditions and one's own surveyor should be able to list the faults of any property and so strengthen the bargaining in one's favour.

Usually it is not possible to borrow the total amount of money needed to buy a home. One has to make a capital contribution oneself. The size of this contribution will depend upon the size of the mortgage raised and the price of the new property.

There are several types of mortgages available, and advice can be sought from the estate agent or from one's own solicitor. Money may be borrowed for this purpose from a bank, a building society, an insurance company, a trust fund or the local authority.

Types of Mortgage Available

Repayment mortgage: This type of mortgage can be repaid over a period of many years (usually about twenty-five). It has the advantage that income tax relief can be claimed on the repayments, although the amount decreases annually.

Endowment mortgages: The loan is made for a certain number of years at the end of which it is paid back through an endowment insurance (life policy) which is arranged to mature at the agreed date. The regular monthly payments which have to be made consist of the premiums on the endowment insurance plus the interest on the mortgage. These repayments also qualify for tax relief.

Option mortgages: These are helpful for people who are not paying more than the standard tax rate and are on a low income. Instead of drawing tax relief the person can opt to pay a lower rate of interest.

Insurance Company Loans: The amounts lent by insurance companies for this purpose vary, but all will be at a fixed rate of interest for the agreed period of the loan.

Trust Funds: Private mortgages through Trust Funds can sometimes be obtained at a lower rate of interest and for an indefinite period. The arrangement is made through solicitors and the length of notice for repayment is agreed in the mortgage.

Local Authorities: With recent financial restraints imposed upon them, local authorities are having to review all activities but some still arrange mortgages at fixed rates of interest. They will often lend on properties not favoured by Building Societies and sometimes they may lend up to 100 per cent of the property price.

The Contract

One's own solicitor should proceed with the contract. He will prepare the draft of conveyance and send it to the seller's solicitor for either approval or amendment. He will also need to find out about town planning changes, building by-laws and rights of way and check on 'encumbrances' on the property such as outstanding death duties etc.

It usually takes about a month to complete the purchase after signing a contract. During this period, the buyer is considered by law to be the owner of the property. It is vital, therefore, that it is insured immediately after the contract has been exchanged. There are some housing associations, private companies and registered charities who build housing for elderly people where an investment is required to purchase a long lease. Details can be obtained from the local authority, the Citizens Advice Bureau, the local Age Concern Group or Age Concern Headquarters.

Tenants (Those living in rented accommodation)

If it is decided to rent a home for one's old age, it is wise to ascertain a number of points concerning the tenancy. It is important, for example, to know whether one is going to be

a protected or an unprotected tenant, whether one is going to
be responsible for repairs and also the laws concerning security of tenure. While various Acts including the Housing
Act 1980 are concerned with security of tenure and the level
of rent of a private tenant (whether the accommodation is
furnished or unfurnished), there is no protection under current Acts for those private tenants whose rent includes payment for board and service.

Security of Tenure

Security of tenure depends upon the category of tenancy
which is mainly determined by whether or not the landlord
lives on the premises. The 1977 Rent Act divided private
tenancies into 'Protected' and 'Statutory' tenancies. Both can
be either regulated or controlled. The 1980 Housing Act created 'Protected Shorthold' tenancies and 'Assured' tenancies.

A Regulated Tenancy

This type of tenancy is subject to the regulations of the
Fair Rent system. Conditions which have to be met are:
   that the dwelling is privately owned;
   that the rateable value of the tenant's part of the property
      is less than £750 outside London, and less than £1,500
      in Greater London;
   that the annual rent is at least two-thirds of the rateable
      value;
   that the landlord either does not live in the dwelling or if
      he does, that the tenancy is an unfurnished one and first
      granted before August 14th 1974.
To have the rent registered or to have a fair rent determined, either the tenant or the landlord or both must apply
to the Rent Officer.
   When a rent has been registered, it stays operative for two
years unless circumstances radically change, such as the property being improved or allowed to deteriorate. (Unless the
rent was registered before 28 November 1980 when it stays
operative for three years until a new registration.)
   If a fair rent is requested, a form has to be completed giving
full details of the tenancy, including the accommodation and
services provided. A figure for an alternative rent must also
be suggested. The rent officer will inspect the property and
discuss the situation with both the tenant and the landlord

before arriving at his decision. If either disagrees with the figure he decides, appeal can be made to a rent assessment committee. Both parties can be represented at this but such hearings do not qualify for legal aid. After hearing the case, the committee will fix a rent.

A Controlled Tenancy: Conversion to Regulation

Any existing tenancy contracted before July 6th 1957 was a controlled tenancy if:

the rateable value on March 31st 1972 was under £35 (£70 in Greater London);

the dwelling was let unfurnished and was privately owned;

the rent was fixed against the 1956 rateable value.

The Housing Act 1980, however, brought to an end all controlled tenancies, converting them to regulated tenancies as above.

Shorthold Tenancies

The Housing Act 1980 created shorthold tenancies, granted for a fixed period of between one and five years, agreed at the beginning of the letting. A fair rent must be registered and the landlord has a mandatory right to take possession at the end of the period as long as certain conditions are complied with.

Assured Tenancies

These are tenancies granted only to landlords who are approved by the Secretary of State. The property must be newly built and the approved landlord can let at a market rent. Tenants have security during the period of their lease but no rent is registered. These tenancies were also created by the 1980 Housing Act.

Protected and Statutory Tenancies

A protected tenancy is a contractual tenancy where the Rent Acts apply. A statutory tenancy exists by Rent Act protection instead of by a written contract.

Before a tenant can be dispossessed or evicted, both protected and statutory tenancies require a valid notice to quit to be issued and a Possession Order granted by the County Court. A notice to quit must include information relating to the tenant's rights. A solicitor will be able to advise or free advice may be obtained either from the local housing aid centre, law centre, or Citizens Advice Bureau. To qualify for protection:

> there must be an existing contract or lease (it is important to acquire this when one first agrees to rent) or the tenant has statutory protection under the Rent Acts;
>
> the property must be let as a separate dwelling;
>
> the rent paid must be over two-thirds of the rateable value of the dwelling.

Where the landlord does not live in the same dwelling as his tenant, the tenancy is known as a protected tenancy and except where the rateable value of the part of the property occupied by the tenant exceeds certain limits, the tenant's rights are protected under the Rent Acts and before he can dispossess (evict) a tenant, the landlord has to acquire a Possession Order from the County Court.

Where the landlord is resident and the tenant shares his home, the tenant is not fully protected unless the accommodation is rented unfurnished and he has lived there since before August 14th 1974, with the landlord sharing neither the kitchen nor the bathroom nor the w.c. An unprotected tenant cannot be evicted unless the landlord obtains a County Court order after serving notice to quit.

Part protection is available to some tenants of resident landlords, depending on the terms of the tenancy. Restricted contracts (i.e. where 'rent' is paid and where substantial boad is not provided) can give extra time in the accommodation according to the date the tenancy began.

> Before 28th November 1980:
>
> > if a notice to quit is issued, the tenant can apply to the Rent Tribunal, before the notice expires, for up to six months extension of stay;
>
> After 28th November 1980:
>
> > there is no suspension of the notice – but the courts can postpone the date when the possession order comes into effect for up to three months.

A Landlord's Responsibilities

One may decide to take a tenant into one's own home in order to have company and share expenses. All the above points concerning tenancies should be read as some will apply, but in addition, it is important to realize that there are responsibilities and to know that help with them can be obtained.

Improvements or Intermediate Grants

Tenants can require a landlord to put adequate facilities into his property, or to repair it.

Where a tenant has a written lease, the repair covenant should state the extent of the tenant's liability. Care must be taken in this, however, as the wording may not be conclusive. Other provisions in the lease may affect its interpretation. When major repairs are needed, the housing aid centre or Citizens Advice Bureau will give advice.

The Housing Act 1980 has enabled private tenants to claim renovation grants themselves. Normally the landlord's permission is required but this cannot be withheld unreasonably. Before applying, however, tenants should check the landlord's responsibilities.

Although a private tenant's right to repairs depend upon the terms of the lease, he can ask his local authority to serve an appropriate notice to his landlord to get certain improvements or repairs carried out (Section 9 of the Housing Act 1957) or can go to the County Court in order to get the work done.

Generally in long leases, the tenant covenants to undertake all repairs, while in short leases, the landlord assumes liability for structural and outside repairs. He is not liable to repair unless he knows of the need. A tenant therefore, should inform his landlord *in writing* as soon as a repair becomes necessary.

It should be remembered that after improvements have been carried out, the landlord can apply to increase the rent.

Leasehold Property

To all intents and purposes, people living in leasehold property under long-term leases, at ground rents, can be categorized as owner-occupiers. Under the Leasehold Reform Act 1967, as amended by recent Housing Acts, certain long leaseholders have the right to buy the freehold of their property, or to extend the lease for 50 years. If a leaseholder does not exercise these rights he or she can, after termination of the lease, remain as a statutory tenant, paying a fair rent. Further details are contained in the leaflet 'Leasehold Reform: A Guide for Leaseholders', available at a Citizens Advice Bureau or from the local town hall.

Death of a Private Tenant

When a tenant dies, his spouse or any member of his family who has been living in the household for (at least) the previous six months is entitled to take over the tenancy. This offers protection to a middle-aged daughter or son who has cared for an aged parent for at least six months before the death occurs.

Allowances and Rebates

Some older people who are tenants of private landlords or of housing associations qualify for a rent allowance. This is dependant upon the size of the income, the amount of rent paid, and also family dependency. Advice on these subjects can be obtained from the housing department of the local authority or from housing advice centres. The Citizens Advice Bureau also have a useful pamphlet on the subject: 'There's Money off Rent'.

Rent Rebate: Rent rebates are granted to council tenants who are eligible. They usually take the form of rent reductions.

Rate Rebate: It is also worth checking whether one qualifies for a rate rebate. This can be done at the Treasurer's Department of the local authority.

Another useful pamphlet, also available from the housing advice centres and council offices, as well as from the local Citizens Advice Bureau, is 'How to pay less Rates'.

Council Tenants

Many local authorities have their own accommodation which they rent to elderly people. Application should be made to the housing department of the local authority of the district in which one wishes to live.

The Housing Act 1980 gave both council and housing association tenants legal rights and details of these are given in 'The Tenants Charter'; 'The Right to Buy'; and 'Housing Association Rents', all obtainable from the Department of the Environment.

Applications for adaptations to the home should be made usually either to the social services department of the local authority or to the domiciliary occupational therapist (the local Citizens Advice Bureau will have names and addresses where the latter exist).

Living With Relations or Friends

At the present time, it is fairly common and socially approved for a married son or daughter to invite an elderly parent to give up his own home and live with them. If there is sufficient space and sufficient physical and financial resources, this may work out well. There are, however, a number of inherent dangers which may not at first be fully appreciated.

First, the old person still loses his home, and the sense of psychological loss together with the need for personal adaptation can be as severe as if he were going into an institution. This is especially true if the neighbourhood is different and contacts and customs of a lifetime are also lost. Second, it can never be certain that the family will be able or willing to continue the arrangement and then the old person, having lost his own home, has no alternative but to go into institutional care. Third, it is almost impossible for the caring relative to resist taking over from the old person, both physically and mentally and to adopt the I'll-do-it-for-you syndrome. The result of this kind of environment has been outlined in a previous chapter. What the old person himself really wants or needs must be looked at objectively and discussed by everyone concerned.

The loss of one's home, however good the reasons for leaving it may be, can be experienced as a form of bereavement and can produce the same grief reaction as the loss of a close relative. In his book, *Loss and Change*, Peter Marris quotes a study of the reactions of families moved, under an urban renewal scheme, from the West End of Boston, in which it was concluded that:

> for the majority it seems quite precise to speak of their reactions as expressions of grief. These are manifest in the feelings of painful loss, the continual longing, the general depressive tone, frequent symptons of psychological or social or somatic distress, the active work required in adapting to the altered situation, the sense of helplessness, the occasional expressions of both direct and displaced anger, and the tendencies to idealise the lost place. At their most extreme, these reactions of grief are intense, deeply felt and, at times, overwhelming.

Marris has gone on to suggest that, like bereavement, a change of home should be understood as 'a potential disruption of the meaning of life'. 'For some', he says, 'it may be a profound disturbance from which they never recover.' The loss is even greater, of course, if, because of lack of space, they have to lose the greater part of their possessions of a lifetime such as favourite pieces of furniture which have been in the family for generations or their own wedding presents. These are not just status symbols, they are reassuring evidence of identity. A good deal of research supports Marris' conclusion and it is clear that such losses are particularly serious for those who are mentally impaired, physically ill or already suffering from depression. These people are unable to make the positive effort which is required to identify with the new life. Gutman and Herbert have quoted thirteen studies which show that the death rate of elderly people is unusually high during the first year of 're-location', and particularly so during the first three months.

Full account also has to be taken of the physical and mental abilities of the family to cope with night disturbances and the possibility of illness or disease. Financial circumstances may change; the breadwinner may be assigned to work in another part of the country; children, unable to have their friends to stay may, if not brought into the initial discussions, resent the old person from the very beginning. The noise and untidiness of young children can also be intolerable to some old people who have to live in close proximity to them. Each family will be able to identify personal circumstances which are likely to occur or alter in their own lives and must identify these areas during their decision making.

Some families decide upon a programme by which the old person spends so many months each year with each of his or her offspring. This is a very unsettling arrangement for most old people and they can feel unwanted and rather hurt as they and their possessions are packed up and spirited off to a new destination. If it can be arranged as six months in the country and six months in town, or the autumn and winter in one place and the spring and summer in another, it will give much more dignity to the scheme, even if only psychologically.

When living with each other is decided upon, it must be exactly that in reality. If host-and-guest roles are adopted it will mean that the old person has no home. If the arrangement is to work, the parent must also feel not only wanted but needed. He or she must have work to do, household duties to undertake and participate completely, so much as he is able, in the running of the *mutual* home. Joint responsibility also brings shared authority and personal pride and dignity. The old person otherwise becomes a recipient and nothing more and such a status, even temporarily held, is intolerable for most of us. For a proud and independent old lady or gentleman it is likely to mean a miserable life until death.

When movement into a shared home *is* decided upon, the step should be prepared for and taken with the seriousness and importance it deserves.

Club Life

Sharing a home does not mean that the old person and his family have to be in each other's pockets all day. Younger members will need to go out and about and it is important for the elderly member to enjoy other environments from time to time. Day centres and luncheon clubs, because they provide some care, are particularly helpful when relatives need to be out of the house for some hours each day. A day centre can, if the old person wishes, provide a meeting place where he or she can see local friends and engage in social activities. His hobby may be catered for and an opportunity offered to indulge in some kind of hand-work or games, such as bridge or bingo, billiards or darts. Some centres are in the form of workshops where elderly pensioners can earn a small sum of money giving them some degree of purpose. Another type of centre provides day-time care. There is full-time supervision and meals are available at a reasonable price. Transport to and from these centres is sometimes provided by volunteers, but for obvious reasons this service has become less frequent of late.

Some voluntary organizations also provide their own afternoon club facilities and in some areas transport to these, to shops, libraries and even to doctors' surgeries is available. Others, if requested, provide a day-relief or a night-sitter service. The local Citizens Advice Bureau or social services department (or representative) and the local branch of Age Concern or the Red Cross should be able to provide information on what is available in the district. Luncheon clubs are an extension of the meals-on-wheels service. Their venue is usually a local community home or hall and more mobile pensioners can buy an inexpensive hot luncheon there. Again, these clubs provide meeting places for friends. Several other social services are available for elderly people all over the country, but their frequency and charges, like the home-help service, vary from one area to another.

Shared Care

A lack of these kind of services in some parts of the country has contributed to a few innovatory practices springing up. Small groups of villagers, flat residents or local householders have come together to share responsibilities for helping those old people who need someone to be with them all the time. With a number of friends and neighbours involved, each person's 'turn' to shop, cook and sit with the old person, or help with washing and bathing comes round to an average of only once in three weeks or so. In these days of shorter working weeks and shorter working days, this does not ask the impossible of anyone. Others invite the elderly parent or friend if they are going to church, for a drive, to the theatre or cinema, to the shops or out for a meal.

Foster Care

Foster care schemes exist in some areas. This means that individuals or families take older people into their own homes as paying guests. Some of these schemes are the responsibility of the social service departments, others are run by voluntary organizations.

The local office of the social service department will advise whether such a scheme exists locally and also whether the 'guest' qualifies for a supplementary pension to help pay the negotiated rates.

Group Living

There are, of course, old people whose homes cannot be adapted or altered to meet their changed needs, and yet they still wish to keep their independence. To achieve this, some families have designed more original plans.

Six families in North London, all with disabled or older

relatives, found that they could not carry out their own work commitments and also give the constant and regular attention required by these scattered family members. Collectively they purchased a house, employed a nurse and a cook and individually guaranteed practical help for one full day each week. It should be emphasized that in each case the decision was reached only after full consultation and discussion with the old person concerned.

Some people have found that a rota, such as that adopted by young parents for ferrying their own and friends' children to and from school, can also be used for older, incapacitated members of a community. The key factor is good organization, after full discussion with everyone concerned.

For old people who have some resources, financial, human or material, other ideas have been put into practice. Some enterprising individuals have 'done their own thing' very successfully. After a good deal of discussion, planning, financial re-arranging, acquisition of loans and/or pooling of family resources, couples have bought a large house and converted it themselves to form individual flats or flatlets for several elderly relatives and one larger flat for themselves and their own young children. (In these days of divorces and re-marriages the number of elderly in-laws, aunts and uncles some people have is in double figures). Whilst keeping their independence and taking responsibility for the care of their own flats, all contribute to certain joint activities, such as shopping, cooking and laundry. Older members of these families have been amazed to find that under such circumstances not only do they become more self-sufficient but they are also able to help young parents with their children. As a result, all lives are made much more interesting.

Granny Annexes

Other families have set up a granny annexe for their elderly relative. This has the advantage of being near to, yet not *with*, the younger members. Usually they take the form of a bungalow erected beside the house or flat of a married child and family. Sometimes they are mobile homes. In both instances, the local planning department must be consulted first.

It is essential to the success of such an arrangement that an independent pattern of living is set up by each household right from the beginning. The minimum required is a bed-sitting room, 'somewhere to cook', and a bathroom and w.c.

Hotel Accommodation
Some hotels in this country specialize in providing accommodation for 'permanent residents'. Usually this consists of a bedroom with use of the communal rooms for meals, television and reading. If this form of home is decided upon, it is important to obtain written assurances from the hotel manager that the room is available all the year round. A disadvantage of this type of accommodation is that usually the staff will not provide care when illness or increasing infirmity necessitates personal attention. Families who have relations in such accommodation need to visit regularly otherwise the old person can feel isolated and sometimes even neglected.

Information on such hotels and guest houses in the south of England is available from Mrs Gould's Residential Advisory Centre for the Elderly (GRACE) and enquiries should be addressed to P.O. Box 71, Cobham, Surrey. All accommodation recommended has been visited by the Centre's staff.

Almshouses
Almshouses are charitably endowed houses providing residential accommodation for persons whose financial circumstances qualify them for acceptance.

Although one is inclined to think that they belong to another age, there are still approximately 23,000 such dwellings in this country. Those who live in them are called residents and not 'almswomen' or 'almsmen' as in the past.

In recent years there has been extensive rebuilding and improving of property, and each almshouse has its individual criteria for selection. Generally, one has to have lived in the area for some time or belong to a particular trade or profession. In each case an application should be made to the appropriate trustees. Information on eligibility for an almshouse can be obtained from the General Secretary, The National Association of Almshouses.

Sheltered Housing

Grouped housing in the form of flats, flatlets or bungalows is provided by some voluntary organizations, private housing societies, and, although new ventures are appearing less often now from this source, by many local authorities. This type of housing aims to give maximum privacy and independence in specially designed or adapted accommodation. Shared facilities, such as a community sitting- or television-room, library, laundry and sick-bay may also be available within the building. The whole is easily maintained, has easy access and contains helpful aids in the kitchens, bathrooms and w.c's. Usually all doorways are wide enough to allow wheelchairs to pass through them, the flooring has non-skid surfaces and the whole building is centrally heated. The warden of the house acts as a contact person in times of emergency but in some houses, if requested to do so, he or she visits or telephones each resident every day. Unfortunately, the availability of this type of accommodation is limited and although some parts of the country are better off than others, most agencies have waiting lists.

Sheltered housing can belong to the local authority or to a housing association. One of its great advantages is the maintenance of independence, for tenants may take their own furniture and they have their own front door.

While modern units are usually self-contained, some of the older sheltered houses require tenants to share bathrooms and w.c.s. Some sheltered houses do not permit pets. Many have a communal sitting room, laundry facilities and a room for residents' overnight visitors. All have a warden who keeps an eye on all residents.

Local Authority Sheltered Housing

Application for local authority sheltered housing should be made early on if one decides this is going to be needed, as most have a waiting list. Owner-occupiers take low priority as the allocation of all housing is determined by need. Some authorities have separate lists or varying criteria for persons over a certain age. In other areas, the residence qualifications are waived if the applicant's family live in the area. One must be prepared to give detailed personal information regarding income and outgoings, and if there is any difficulty in completing any section of the form, the housing officer will usually help. If there is urgency because of illness or unsuitable housing, a doctor's letter confirming the illness or special needs should be attached to the application form.

Housing Associations' Sheltered Housing

Tenants for housing association dwellings are usually selected according to their housing needs and the individual association's criteria. Housing associations are either registered or unregistered.

A list of associations providing sheltered housing can be obtained from the National Federation of Housing Associations, or from a local branch of Age Concern, a housing advice centre or the local authority housing department, whose addresses will be in the local telephone directory. If the need is urgent, the social worker of the local authority should be contacted.

Old People's Homes

Under this heading come rest homes, residential homes and communal homes. None is meant to provide nursing care and indeed most will require residents to lead a fairly independent life. The amount of care given varies: most will provide help with washing and dressing, feeding and mobility, but most will not take people who are confined to wheelchairs or are incontinent.

When choosing such a home, it is important to bear in mind the distance from the shops, post office, church, public transport and pub, and also the type of residents already living there. Enquiries should also be made as to whether one can have one's own furniture or small personal possessions. Some homes will take married couples.

The Purpose of a Home

Ideally, all old people's homes should have certain features. Living units should be small, with the sexes integrated and be situated within the usual residential areas of the community. They should ensure the maximum participation of residents in the running of their daily lives.

Practical implications of this policy include emphasis on maintaining as much self-care and independence as possible. An old lady, for example, should continue to maintain her customary involvement in the community, go to the local hairdresser, attend her usual church and enjoy the cinema or concerts, and as late at night as she wishes. Once such extra-mural interests are lost, it is almost impossible to reawaken them again.

The Centre for Policy on Ageing has become deeply involved in the problems and possibilities of improving standards of residential care for the elderly. It is 'especially concerned to ensure that right and proper emphasis on improving the quality and quantity of domiciliary care and providing proper support for caring friends and relatives is not seen as an alternative to raising the quality and quantity of residential provision.' The two services are seen as complementary:

> If homes can offer day and weekend care; temporary 'half-way' care on discharge from hospital; short-stay support in times of family crisis, temporary disability or other urgent need, and rehabilitation after bereavement, self/ neglect or illness, they will become part of the supportive network which enables elderly people to stay independent for as long as possible and enables neighbours and friends to sustain a caring role.

All old people's homes should give the very frail and the mentally or physically disabled old person a setting in which he or she is treated as a recognized and respected individual with a long and complex personal history and with his or her own emotional needs, personal tastes, hopes, fears and foibles.

Deciding on Residential Care

If we look at the reasons given by most people who have an elderly relation in a long-term home, it is clear that very rarely does a carefully thought out assessment of alternatives take place before admission is arranged. More often it is an 'arbitrary response to social fears and pressures or the failure of social support'. While the hospital patient is only in danger of becoming 'long-stay', the resident in an old person's home is virtually certain to become so. Once admitted to 'care', there is little hope of returning to independence. And many old people realize this. Often they agree to the move because they 'don't want to be a burden'.

It must be quite clear to all concerned why such a move is

being mooted. The relatives should ask themselves whether they are taking the action because they are afraid that they will incur criticism if an accident occurs when the old person is living alone. They may find their feelings of guilt assuaged if a health or social service worker suggests that the old person has a right to live as she likes, and that if she wants to take a risk, it is up to her.

Before deciding on admission to residential care, it is important to seek a medical assessment to discover whether the mental or physical condition which is causing concern represents 'the last straw'. Confusion, for example, has many causes and its effects can often be dealt with by simple means. Self-neglect, because of depression or over enthusiastic medication, can also result in unnecessary admission to an institution.

Other circumstances which sometimes influence the decision to move the old person into institutional care include discharge from hospital after treatment or for investigations. Hospital staff often discharge patients as soon as possible because of the pressure on acute hospital beds. The old person may have become dependent upon others during his stay in hospital and lost confidence to live by himself. At any age, it takes time to readjust and to fend for oneself after a spell in hospital. Patience and gradual weaning are often effective.

Entering an Old People's Home

After assessment, the possible application to a home must be discussed fully with the potential resident. The person should have all the facts given to him or her, have the opportunity to visit the prospective new home and know exactly what he or she is deciding upon. Taking someone from their own home for the rest of their life is a very serious step, and friends and relations as well as the staff of the residential home share an enormous responsibility. All too frequently they do not face up to it. A chart setting out 'good practice' in this field is given on pp. 58–61.

Private and Voluntary Residential Homes

Admission to a private home is usually controlled by the trustees, governing body or staff members. Criteria are likely to relate to the financial circumstances and physical condition of the applicant. Most will not accept people with any mental illness.

Charges can be high. Requests for financial assistance for fees should be made to the social services department before admission is arranged as it is essential to ensure that long-term financial resources are available.

Some charitable organizations run homes themselves and will also make grants towards private home fees. There are several who will sponsor ill or discharged ex-Service men and women for example, while the charitable work for some livery companies includes help for those from relevant trades or occupations.

Local authorities keep lists of private and voluntary homes within their areas and have a duty to ensure that standards do not fall before 'the specified level'. Further information may be obtained from Counsel and Care for the Elderly.

Local Authorities' Homes

Applications for admission to one of these homes should be made through the social services department of the local authority. The application will contain questions relating to past and present circumstances, physical defects (especially those of mobility, hearing and sight), degree of dependence and some legal aspects such as the existence of a will, name of solicitor and any insurance policies held. Financial circumstances will also be discussed and information will have to be given concerning retirement and occupational pensions, social security benefits, investment interest and any property owned.

Most local authority homes have a waiting list. When a vacancy arises, it should be taken up within a few days.

All local authorities have standard charges for residential accommodation. This is based on the running expenses of a home and the amount the resident is expected to contribute is based upon the assessment of his or her financial resources.

The amount of state retirement pension residents of local authority homes are allowed to keep to cover personal expenses is a Government decision. A minimum fee is laid down as is the difference between the money allowed for personal use and the retirement pension. A supplementary pension may be claimed if necessary. If one has an income greater than the basic retirement pension or capital assets, a higher fee may be charged.

The practice of admissions

Phase	Duration	Focus of work	Elements
			1 The application
I Preparation	From the time that an application for residential care is made up to the notification that a place is available.	Assessment and preparation of the prospective resident for life in residential care.	2 Its outcome
			3 The choice of home
			1 Notification
II Separation	From the notification that a place is available to the moment of admission.	Achieving a smooth transition from community to residential life.	2 Confirmation
			3 Separation
			4 Transportation

The practice of admissions

Activities	*Implications*
Assessing the background to the application and the prospective resident. Exchanging basic information about the likely cost of residential care, its location and lifestyle.	A wide ranging assessment that includes home, social and psychological factors places the application in the context whereby the full needs rather than just the presenting ones can be evaluated. It will provide the basis for accepting or rejecting the application and developing the guidelines for ongoing work in community and/or residential care.
Personal notification to the prospective resident of the outcome.	Acceptance of the application implies a level of need that justifies ongoing work in the interim period. In other cases preventive work may be appropriate.
Giving prospective residents sufficient information upon which they may base 'choice' and anticipate meaningfully the life in an old people's home.	The opportunity should be provided for prospective residents to visit homes for single days and weekends. Preparation for changes in lifestyle begins.
Informing the prospective resident personally of the home in which they are invited to live, its address, facilities, etc.	Information about the personal belongings, clothes, etc., that will be needed/can be taken to the home is passed on. Consultation about the remaining property, pets, etc., is begun.
Confirmation of the initial application and deciding upon a mutually convenient date for admission.	Sufficient time should be allowed to complete admission arrangements satisfactorily.
Saying farewell to neighbours, friends, etc., ensuring that at the same time, they know of the new address	Consider working with families of newly admitted residents to ensure visiting. Encourage the maintenance of links with the community.
Deciding with relatives, etc., the transfer arrangements, allowing sufficient time for it to be unhurried, sufficient space for personal belongings to be taken.	The continuity of contact between the social worker and the prospective resident should be maintained from the assessments and notification phases through to residential life itself.

The practice of admissions

Phase	Duration	Focus of work	Elements
III Transition	The first day in the new home.	Ensuring that the impact of the change in life between the community and residential home is managed sympathetically.	First meetings with: 1 Officer in charge 2 Staff 3 Residents 4 Routines 5 Physical environment
IV Incorporation	From the end of the first day until the new resident looks on the home as 'home'.	Development of the resident's interests and life in the new home and in the community.	1 Development of new 'anticipations'
			2 Retaining existing social links and developing others.

If assets are not realizable (such as a house in which the family is living), an agreement may be entered into whereby when the property is sold, the local authority can claim a sum equal to the accumulated debt. For further information the housing department or the social worker at the local authority should be contacted.

Nursing Homes

The official definition of a nursing home in this country is 'any premises used or intended to be used for the reception of, and providing nursing for, persons suffering from injury or infirmity'. The 'premises' must be under the charge of a resident of the home, who will be either a registered medical practitioner or a registered nurse. There must also be a proportion of qualified nurses employed by the home to care for their patients.

All such homes are required to register with and be regulated by the health authority. Supervision is usually the joint

The practice of admissions

Activities	Implications
Arranging the most appropriate time to arrive at the home and creating an atmosphere where the introductions can be made most naturally. Ensuring that the new resident knows her way around the home and to whom to turn for advice, support and understanding.	Field and residential staff need to work together to co-ordinate their roles during the admission. Existing residents/staff in the home who may already know resident or her home area could be introduced to her. Choice of 'key worker' in the home.
Formulation of a programme for residential care.	Working with the new resident to understand the impact of the change in life. Identifying the areas of stress and of development.
Ensuring that the resident enjoys as full and as satisfying a life as can be provided.	Working with others in the community, the home and the social services department as a whole to meet the interests of residents.

Source: P. Pope, 'Admission to Residential Homes for the Elderly', *Social Work Today* Vol. 9. No. 44 July 18 1978. Reproduced with permission.

responsibility of the nursing officer for local authority liaison and the community health physician and social services.

Most homes have certain criteria regarding the patients they admit. Some will not take those who are blind, others will not take those suffering from a progressive disorder and so on. Information on nursing homes can be obtained from The Registered Nursing Homes Association, the Centre for Policy on Ageing or Counsel and Care for the Elderly, and on short stay homes from the local Age Concern group, Citizens Advice Bureau, local authority or The National Council for the Single Woman and her Dependants. Not all homes can be recommended and great care should be taken when choosing one.

Settling to a New Life Pattern

The settling down to a new chapter of life is sometimes made more difficult if some degree of sensory deprivation is present, such as deafness or difficulty in seeing. Normally, an individual orientates himself to new surroundings by the reception of information through the sense organs and the reception of these stimuli by the brain. Research studies have found that although elderly individuals vary in their ability to cope with an altered sensory environment and their reaction to it, a number of disturbances frequently occur. For example, emotional changes may include anxiety. There may be disturbances in thinking ability, including difficulty in maintaining an ordered sequence of thoughts. As a result, unusual, even bizarre ideas may be expressed. Derangements may occur, ranging from mild day-dreaming to more severe illusions and hallucinations. The latter may involve seeing people or animals, hearing voices or feeling one's body rising and falling. These manifestations can be better dealt with if understood, and the family or friends involved should ask the primary health care team for advice and guidance.

Clearly, the state of one's financial circumstances becomes a most important factor in deciding where and how to live. For most people a reduced income will accompany old age so it is particularly important to ensure that one is receiving all benefits to which one is entitled, and that one is investing capital wisely. While full advice is available only from experts, the following chapter gives brief guidance on how to obtain assistance and where to go for financial help.

CHAPTER 5

CONTROLLING FINANCIAL AND LEGAL AFFAIRS

Wine maketh merry; but money answereth all things.

Ecclesiastes 10:19

At any age, how and where one lives, as well as the state of one's physical and mental well-being, are influenced by one's income. For the majority of us, the inevitable reduction in income which occurs when leaving full-time gainful employment means that money and all matters connected with it become even more important then heretofore. Many of us have to make some kind of adjustment in life-style; it may not be as drastic a step as changing homes, but it will certainly entail some detailed, albeit reluctant, consideration of incomings and outgoings. Before accepting a fixed income as unalterable it is worth-while to consider some ways of supplementing it. For general advice on investments, annuities and tax, the bank manager is usually the best person to consult. For information regarding specific entitlements from the State, a Citizens Advice Bureau or the department of social security should be contacted. In either case, a general brief idea of what one is talking about will increase the value of an interview or discussion.

Investment of Capital, Retirement or Redundancy Pay
Annuities

An annuity may be bought (usually from an insurance company) either by regular small payments or by a single payment. The latter is usually recommended for older people because the older the person, the higher the annual income from payment. There are considerable variations in the terms offered by companies. An additional benefit of an annuity is that only part of the income from it is subject to tax; a fraction is calculated by the company and is regarded as a return of one's capital. This fraction is determined by the purchaser's age but is usually more than one half. If an annuity is purchased on behalf of a couple, the income continues for as long as one of them is living. One major disadvantage of an annuity is that capital is expended with the purchase and so cannot be willed to another or recovered.

Bank Deposit Accounts

The rates of interest on these vary from time to time. Interest is taxable. Seven days' notice of withdrawal is required.

Building Societies

If one is liable to tax at the standard rate, investment in a building society can offer a good return. The society pays tax so the interest paid to an investor is net of basic rate income tax.

Government Securities

The advantages of investment in these securities are that they pay a higher rate of interest than almost all others and when bought through a bank or broker, can be converted into cash at short notice. Their value is not fixed however, so money can be lost if one has to sell when their value is low. On the other hand, as with the other types of shares, one can also make a profit by selling when their value is high. If such gains or losses are made more than twelve months after purchase, they are exempt from capital gains tax. The government promises to repay, usually at a specified agree date, the money invested and in the meantime pays interest on the loan it has received. That interest is taxable. Further information is given in the pamphlet 'Government Stock' available from post offices and banks.

Index-Linked National Savings Certificates

The purchase of these is no longer restricted to those over the age of 50. The maximum worth one can hold is £5000. They are linked to the Retail Price Index and therefore are inflation proof. The 'maturity-age' is five years; after that time one receives the purchase price, plus the inflation-linked increase, plus a bonus of 4 per cent on the purchase price.

The inflation-linked increase is exempt from income tax, investment surcharge and capital transfer tax. If inflation is high, these certificates are a good investment.

National Giro

This is a low-cost current-account banking service which is aimed to facilitate saving and also to make payments (or cash withdrawals if necessary). Transfer can be arranged to pay a certain sum regularly to other Giro account holders, such as TV rental firms, and to make payments such as insurance, rates, mortgage repayments and other bills, which may include electricity, gas and telephone as well as those from large stores. One can also apply for loans from the Mercantile Credit Company Ltd. (Branch telephone numbers and addresses will be in the local telephone directory.) Further information is given in 'National Giro Fees and Stationery Charges', available at post offices.

National Savings Certificates

These are also a Government Security. The State is directly responsible for the repayment of capital in full, or in the case of an index-linked certificate, for the payment of the total value of the capital plus any bonus due. Each certificate costs £10 and increases in value over a period of five years. Money and interest may be withdrawn at any time but it may be more than eight clear days before the money is received. Further information is contained in leaflet P.156W obtainable from post offices and banks.

National Savings Bank (Post Office)

Ordinary Accounts: very small amounts (the minimum is 25 pence) can be deposited in a Post Office Savings Bank account. Normally interest is paid annually. The rate of interest may change but the value of the original deposit remains the same. The first £70 (per annum) of interest is tax free. Small withdrawals can be made at any time but for withdrawals of over £50 special application forms must be completed.

Investment Accounts: These pay a higher rate of interest. Again this is fluctuating in the present economic climate, but one month's notice must be given for withdrawal of any money.

Shares

A bank manager or stockbroker's advice should be sought if a large amount of money is to be invested. Speculative investing on the stockmarket can end in disaster and expert advice should be obtained before any shares are bought.

Loans
Maturity Loans

If money is required for work to one's home, a maturity loan may be sought. Contact should be made with the staff at the housing advice centre of the local housing authority who will be able to advise. One advantage of this loan is that usually the capital does not have to be paid back during the borrower's lifetime. As it will be rendered on the death of the borrower however, it is in the interests of the surviving spouse for the property to be in joint ownership or take out an insurance policy so that the loan can be continued during his or her lifetime. Interest has to be paid for the period of the loan. Since October 1980 local authorities have been required to charge interest at a rate specified by the Secretary of State; which reflects the rates currently being charged by building societies. This is called 'standard national rate' (S.N.R.). Those local authorities whose costs of financing loans exceed S.N.R. must charge at a higher rate. Alternatively the rate of interest may be calculated at the option mortgage rate. People who receive supplementary pensions can apply for an increase in these to cover their interest payments. A disadvantage of this kind of loan is that the interests of beneficiaries under a will can be adversely affected.

Mortgage Annuities

If one has a reasonably high income but little capital apart from one's home it may be possible to benefit from a mortgage annuity. Under this agreement, an elderly owner-occupier takes out a mortgage loan up to 75 per cent of the value of his house and with the loan, purchases an annuity to bring in a fixed income for the rest of his life. Increased annuity payments may be arranged as the house increases in value because of inflation. The loan is repaid on death, usually from the proceeds of the sale of the house. Disadvantages are that many annuities are not inflation-proofed and also the possession of an annuity can affect one's supplementary pension rights. Further information can be obtained from the Mortgage Brokers' Association.

Benefits and Allowances
Pensions
The retirement pension in this country is payable in an amount based on one's national insurance contributions and earnings since 1978. The pension is taxable.

Criteria for Qualification for Retirement Pension
The person must have:
reached the required age (sixty for a woman and sixty-five for a man);
declared and had accepted by the department of health and social security (DHSS) his or her intention to retire on a specified date;
paid national insurance contributions to a sufficient level.
After the age of sixty-five (for women) or seventy (for men) has been reached a pension is not reduced by earnings. A case where national insurance payments have been made intermittently will usually result in a reduced sum being paid out as retirement pension. An earnings-related pension is based on earnings from April 1978, the date when the 'new' pension scheme came into operation in this country. A married woman who reached the age of 60 before 6 April 1979 is entitled to receive either a pension on her own contributions or on the contributions made by her husband. If she reached 60 on or after 6 April 1979 she may combine the two pensions up to a maximum of the married woman's rate of pension. While the married woman's pension can be paid only when the husband is also drawing his own pension if a woman has paid her own contributions she can claim her pension even though her husband is not drawing his. Further information is contained in a booklet 'Your Rights', available from the local branch of Age Concern.

Pension Scheme for Carers at Home

The new pension scheme also covers a person looking after another at home. Home responsibilities protection is available when a minimum of thirty-five hours a week for the whole tax year is spent in giving care to someone who is receiving an attendance or constant attendance allowance throughout that same year. It is also payable to those who have received supplementary benefit, in order to be able to care for an elderly (or sick) person at home or if child benefit is received for a child under 16. It is necessary to continue to pay Class III contributions (voluntary) if the cared-for does not receive an attendance allowance or the carer does not receive supplementary benefit and home responsibilities protection is not given. (If the carer receives Invalid Care Allowance, he or she is automatically credited with national insurance contributions and need not make a claim.) An exception is made when the carer is within five years of pension age and may have already made an adequate number of contributions to qualify for the retirement pension. If there is any difficulty, the local social security office should be contacted.

Occupation Pension Schemes

There are three main schemes in operation in this country:
  i) The final-salary scheme. This works on the assumption that earnings are at their height in the years immediately preceding retirement. To determine the size of pension, a fraction (usually one-sixtieth or one-eightieth) of the final salary for each year of employment is used.
  ii) The money purchase scheme. This invests the member's contribution through an insurance company. He or she is provided with a pension according to his or her contributions.
  iii) The average-pay scheme. This provides a pension related to year-by-year pay.

The maximum pension on retirement allowed by the Inland Revenue is two-thirds of the final salary.

Over 80s Pension

This pension is non-contributory and is for persons aged eighty or more who do not qualify for the basic retirement pension or receive a retirement pension of less than the amount of the over 80s pension.

Criterion for Qualification for Over 80s Pension
The person must have been living in the UK (or another Common Market country) for ten years since his sixtieth birthday. There are special arrangements for women who were eighty-seven or over and men who were ninety-two or over on July 5th 1975. The local social security office will be able to supply information.

A Widow's Benefits
There are taxable benefits which can be paid to a widow. These are based on her late husband's national insurance contributions.
A Widow's Allowance: This is a resettlement benefit which is paid to a widow for the first twenty-six weeks following the death of her husband. A woman of sixty or over qualifies only if her husband did not qualify for a retirement pension.
A Widowed Mother's Allowance: A widowed mother's allowance is usually payable to a widow with a qualifying child when her widow's allowance ends. The allowance can be paid without increases for children, if the widow has a son or daughter living with her who is under the age of nineteen and has left school. The rate may be reduced if the husband's national insurance contributions have not met the qualifying total.
A Widow's Pension: This is payable when:
   The widow's allowance ends and the widow does not qualify for the widowed mother's allowance and she was forty years old or more when her husband died;
   The widowed mother's allowance ends and the widow is forty years old or more at that time.
Reduced rates are paid to women widowed when they are between the ages of forty and fifty. These rates may be further reduced if the husband's national insurance contributions only partially satisfy the conditions. A widow's benefit ceases if she remarries or lives with a man as his wife.
In order to claim a widow's benefit, the form at the back of the death registration certificate (issued by the registrar of deaths at the time of registering the husband's death) should be completed and sent to the local social security office. Upon

receipt of this the office will issue a claim form which should be completed and returned as soon as possible.

Following a claim, the amount payable is decided by an insurance officer at the local social security office. The office then notifies the claimant of the decision. Additional information can be obtained from the local social security office or from the local branch of Age Concern.

Supplementary Benefits

These are non-contributory benefits available to those whose incomes are considered inadequate to meet their 'requirements' as laid down by the government. Payments are equal to the amount by which the 'income resources' fall short of 'requirements'. These vary according to circumstances.

Criteria for Qualification for Supplementary Benefit Allowance:
    The person must:
    be resident in the UK;
    be at least sixteen years of age and not at school;
    not be in full-time employment;
    normally have registered for work if under pensionable age;
        and have an income which does not satisfy 'requirements'
        as laid down by Parliament.
A person's 'requirements' are made up of the appropriate supplementary benefit scale rate plus an addition for housing requirements (e.g. rent, rates, water rates or equivalent). Additions may also be made to meet special expenses. These are added whenever there are special needs such as diets, domestic help (but not home helps provided by the local authority), travelling expense to and from hospital, laundry and heating. A 'special need' will be considered and recognized on an individual basis if considered to be just that. The amount of weekly benefit is calculated by subtracting the claimant's 'resources' from the 'requirements' figure as determined by the claimant's personal circumstances. In addition to the weekly payments the Supplementary Benefits Commission makes lump-sum payments for certain exceptional needs.

Criteria for Qualification for Single Payments

> The need must be exceptional. (Regulations spell out in detail what is considered 'exceptional');
>
> the claimant's savings must be less than £300 (If they are more than £300 but not enough to pay for whatever is needed, the single payment will be the difference between the amount needed and the savings over £300.);
>
> the claimant is not fully employed.
>
> the claimant must be receiving weekly supplementary benefit or would be entitled to receive supplementary benefit immediately if he or she claimed.

In certain circumstances payment may be obtained for footwear, clothing, bedding, furniture, other essential household equipment, fuel debts, removal expenses and, very exceptionally, hire purchase debts and rent arrears.

Other Benefits

The recipient of supplementary benefit is automatically entitled to other benefits such as free fares to hospital, free dental treatment, spectacles and sometimes legal advice. Others may qualify for help on grounds of low income. Further information is contained in leaflet M.11 entitled 'Free! if you're on a low income: dental treatment, glasses, milk and vitamins, prescriptions', obtainable from post offices and the local social security office.

Attendance Allowance

This is also a non-contributory and non-means-tested allowance. It is tax-free and available for those who are physically and/or mentally disabled and who are unable (and who have been unable over the past six months) to look after themselves.

Criteria for Qualification for Attendance Allowance

> The claimant must:
>
> have been a resident of the UK and have resided there for at least twenty-six weeks out of the past twelve months;
>
> be so severely disabled that he or she needs frequent attention and help with normal bodily functions or continual supervision in order to avoid injury to self or others.

Payment is by order book and is usually combined with state

pension orders. Further information and the necessary claim form are available from the local social security office.

Invalid Care Allowance (ICA)

This is another non-contributary non-means-tested benefit for those who cannot work because they are caring for a severely disabled relative. This benefit is not taxable. For the purposes of this allowance, a person is classified as 'severely disabled' if she or he receives:

the attendance allowance;

the constant attendance allowance paid with a war pension;

industrial injury or disablement pension;

workmen's compensation or equivalent benefit.

Criteria for Qualification for Invalid Care Allowance

The claimant must be:

aged between sixteen and sixty if a woman and between sixteen and sixty-five if a man;

a resident of the UK;

spending at least thirty-five hours a week caring for the relative or friend.

A person is ineligible if:

she is a woman living with her husband or common law husband;

he or she receives the same amount (or more) from some other basic benefit (such as retirement pension, sickness, invalidity or unemployment benefit);

he or she is earning more than £6 per week.

As the ICA is not means-tested it is available to persons receiving supplementary benefit but the supplementary benefit is then reduced by the amount of the ICA. And advantage is that ICA carries credit for national insurance contributions. Further information is given in the leaflet 'Invalid Care Allowance' which is obtainable from the local social security office.

Mobility Allowance

This is a non-means-tested cash payment made to help increase the outdoor mobility of severely disabled people *of working age*. A man or woman receiving mobility allowance when under 66 can continue to receive it until the age of 75 providing qualifying conditions are fulfilled. It is subject to tax. This allowance can also be useful for those old people who have a younger but disabled spouse. Further information is available from the local social security office.

Industrial Disablement Benefit

This is also a non-contributory benefit. It is not taxable and may take the form of either a lump-sum payment or a pension. It is payable to those who, *as a consequence of their work*, have suffered an accidental injury or have contracted a disease as a result of which he or she has a permanent disability.

Criteria for Qualification for Industrial Disablement Benefit

The person must show that the disability is due to work or happened during work. (In the case of injury a record of the place and time it occurred should be produced.)

The injury must have occurred at least twenty-six weeks before the claim is made (industrial injuries benefit will be paid during those twenty-six weeks).

Industrial Injuries Benefit

This is payable for a maximum period of twenty-six weeks from the date either of an accident occurring in the course of paid employment or the development of an industrial disease due to employment. It is paid for *incapacity* due to the injury or disease. Assessment is made by a medical board. Following this the decision regarding the amount to be paid is made by an insurance officer. The amount can be increased if the person qualifies for any of the following allowances:

   special hardship;
   constant attendance;
   hospital treatment;
   unemployability supplement; or very severe disablement.

Further information can be obtained from the local social security office.

War Disablement Pension

This is available to someone who has a disability due wholly or partly to service in the armed forces or as a result of war injury. People eligible are those with a disability:

   resulting from military service in the first world war or since September 1939;

resulting from service in the Merchant Navy during either
the 1914–18 or the 1939–45 war;

resulting from injury due to enemy action received as a
civilian in the 1939–45 war.

A war pension can also be paid to the widow or dependents
of a person who qualified for one before death. The amount
payable varies according to the degree of disability and also,
in the case of Service personnel, to the rank held. Further
information can be obtained from the leaflet 'War Pensions
and Allowances' or direct from the War Pensions Welfare
Service, the ex-Services War Disabled Help and Homes Department, the British Legion or the Citizens Advice Bureau.

Legal Advice and Aid

There is a system in this country called 'fixed fee interviews'
through which some solicitors will give an initial half-hour
interview for £5 (including VAT). People who are receiving
a supplementary pension or who have small capitals and
incomes may obtain free or low-cost legal advice and legal
aid.

The 'Green Form' scheme enables certain persons to obtain
free or inexpensive solicitor's advice for drawing up a will or
where there is a dispute between landlord and tenant. Further
information can be obtained from the legal advice centre, the
law centre, or the Citizens Advice Bureau.

Legal Advice Centres

These are usually run by volunteer lawyers. They are open
only at specific times. Legal advice as well as help with
writing certain letters may be given but usually the lawyers
will not take on court actions. It is necessary to telephone for
an appointment.

Law Centres

These are open during normal office hours and some evenings for those who are resident in the neighbourhood. The
advice given is free of charge and includes court actions with
or without legal aid.

Citizens Advice Bureaux

Some CABs have 'honorary legal advisers' who are local solicitors working on a rota system. Interviews are usually by appointment and are free. These solicitors are allowed to transfer cases to their own offices if necessary and the client is then responsible for the payment of charges. These may be recoverable by legal aid.

Legal Aid

To support legal representation a solicitor may apply to the Law Society on his client's behalf. The local department of health and social security office will check the person's income and savings in order to ascertain that he or she qualifies and inform the Law Society accordingly. The Law Society then decides whether or not the case should be supported by public funds. In either case the applicant is likely to be asked to make some contribution.

Insurance

Life Insurances

These policies are available under:
term insurance;
endowment insurance;
whole life assurance.

Term Insurance: This covers a person against death within a pre-selected period. If the insured person survives longer than that period, no money is refunded.

Endowment Insurance: This covers a person until the end of the pre-selected term or until his or her death (if at an earlier date). Payment is made by the company.

Whole Life Assurance: In this scheme the sum assured is paid when the person dies.

The main disadvantage of an insurance policy is that one's money is no longer accessible until the policy matures or is payable. For this reason not *all* one's savings should ever be put into a life insurance.

Possession Insurance

The replacement value of all personal effects or 'goods and chattels' should be assessed and insured with a reputable company. A house should be insured to cover full rebuilding costs. Policies should be reviewed periodically because of inflation and also when one acquires additional possessions.

Personal Injuries Insurance

Home-owner's policies cover injuries which occur in one's own dwelling. Insurance against personal injury can also be taken out when travelling.

Private Insurance for Illness

There are four main societies which run schemes to cover private medical treatment:

British United Provident Association;
Private Patients Scheme;
Provident Association for Medical Care;
Western Provident Association.

Each scheme covers different circumstances and it is wise to obtain information on all before making a choice.

Legal Fees Insurance

This covers any legal fees which one may incur either by bringing or defending legal action. The policy can be arranged through the DAS Legal Expenses Co.

Taxes

Capital Transfer Tax

This tax acts as a gift tax and estate duty. It applies to gifts a person has made during his lifetime as well as to possessions left on his death. (When a person dies he is considered to 'give away' everything he owns.) There are gifts which are:

tax-free whenever they are given;
tax-free only if made on death;
tax-free only if given during life.

Tax-free gifts include:

gifts from a spouse;
the first £200,000 of gifts made to charities; £100,000 to political parties; passing on of a business (up to £100,000 value);
gifts to specified national institutions;
treasury-approved gifts such as works of art.

Gifts tax-free on death only are:
  'reasonable' funeral expenses;
  lump sums paid to dependants from a person's pension scheme upon his death.
Gifts tax-free during life include:
  gifts from income which represent part of usual spending, (the proviso is that the donor can still keep up his or her normal standard of living out of income);
  gifts of up to £250 to any number of people in each tax year;
  gifts made to maintain any of one's own or one's wife's infirm relations or to maintain a widowed, separated or divorced mother or mother-in-law;
  wedding gifts of up to: £5,000 (if parent of bride or groom), £2,500 (if grandparent or great-grandparent of bride or groom), £1,000 (for all other persons);
  gifts worth up to £3,000 during any tax year (which are not otherwise tax-free).
Further information including how much tax is due, whom to notify when taxable gifts are made and within what period one must pay the tax, can be obtained from one of the capital taxes offices. There are several ways in which capital transfer tax can be saved and the local Citizens Advice Bureau should be able to give advice.

Wills

Those who are unable to consult a solicitor about making a will, may obtain will forms from Oyez Publishing Ltd. A will must be in writing and signed at the end by the person making the will (the testator) in the presence of two witnesses, all three of whom are present *at the same time*. Any alteration made in the will must be signed and witnessed in the same way. If not, the will may be considered invalid.

A will or codicil may be revoked by another will or codicil or by destruction or by marriage. That revocation may be conditional. For a will to be revoked by destruction it must be burned, torn or otherwise destroyed by the testator or by some other person in his presence, and on his instruction and with the intention of revoking it. A legacy or bequest lapses if the beneficiary dies before the testator.

If a person dies without having made an effective will, all property is held in trust for sale. Out of this sum of money the personal representative pays all funeral and administration of estate expenses, debts and other liabilities. The remainder goes to persons said to be beneficially entitled.

Widows and widowers have equal rights but they vary according to the categories of other surviving members of the intestate's family. A widow or widower has the first claim to administer the estate. Unless the estate is very small, Letters of Administration will have to be taken out. One's own solicitor or a local law centre will advise.

Probate

The two executors named in a will are responsible for administering the estate of the person who has died. This means that they must gather the assets, pay taxes and debts, and distribute the remainder (the residue) according to the terms of the will. Usually executors apply for a grant of probate. Some assets can be handed over to executors only on production of probate. This can be obtained from the Probate Registry (address will be in the local telephone directory). The probate office will be able to give helpful advice.

Other Information and Advice.

Because in the '80s the social and economic circumstances of older people are even less favourable than those of people in middle and younger years, a number of national organizations, many with local branches, have arisen to give assistance to and to argue the case for pensioners. Some of these are listed in the Appendix of this book.

But while it would seem true to say that now more than ever before old age is a quality of circumstance, it is also true that it remains a quality of character and is or should be a continuation of being oneself. How one can maintain one's personality, indeed go on to develop it in old age, is a subject deserving considerable thought and discussion. The following chapter attempts to offer some guidelines in this area.

CHAPTER 6

CONTINUING TO BE ONESELF

Old age is not only a quality of character; it is a quality of circumstance. Old Charlie is still the Charles who was top of his class, wrote passionate love letters, won a celebrated court case. . . . Old Charlie's wife is still the woman whose beautiful hair was the envy of her contemporaries, who nearly married a famous man and learned a profession she never had much chance to practice. If memory now plays tricks on them, if their legs will not always carry them where they want to go, if the famous lover is long dead, and the court case relegated to a footnote in legal textbooks, that does not make them different people with a different conception of themselves and different attachments. . . . It only obliges them to find new ways of being themselves.

'Conservatism, Innovation and Old Age'
Peter Marris (unpublished paper) University of California

In his paper Peter Marris goes on to say:

while we impose old age on people, as if it were a meaningful identity, we also talk as if it should not exist at all, as if the ideal were to preserve the identity of a vigorous middle-age to the last, to defy ageing and collude in a conspiracy of silence over its inevitable encroachments. This makes old age a lost cause – a gallant refusal to surrender in the face of repeated setbacks.

How then can people make sense of their lives in old age without either denying the reality of ageing or losing themselves in the spurious identity of a 'senior citizen'? How can they reinterpret the purposes and attachments of an active life, so as to perform another and probably more constricted range of occupations?

Marris, argues Alison Norman in 'Rights and Risk: A Discussion Document on Civil Liberty in old Age', has no simple answer, but he urges us to understand that old age is not a single crisis but a series of events, which are only cumulatively critical; we are only likely to come to terms with these changes and make sense of being old if we recognize that we begin to age almost as soon as we are fully adult and that ageing and dying are part of everyday life. Only then can we give full weight to old people's perceptions of their own identities, their situations, resources, needs and wishes, and cease to impose our stereotypes of age upon them.

The gradual slowing-down that comes with ageing is undeniable. And it need not be denied: a life of hectic activity does not necessarily mean a life with a purpose. Quite frequently it is the opposite. Many young people have recently realized this and have slowed down voluntarily; some have given up high-powered and executive jobs to farm or to market-garden in the country. Others have taken to the sea or gone to live in self-sufficient communities; some have been forced to slow down from the excessive rush and bustle of the twentieth century because of heart attacks or stomach ulcers.

Leisure is an attitude to life, a positive attitude which does not have to be kept waiting until retirement before it is developed. One man's work, that of a professional cricketer, fisherman or carpenter, can be another man's leisure. The distinction between the two lies in the attitude of others towards him and his activity. Leisure is very much linked to the image we have of ourselves. Some of us see ourselves as lone-rangers; we go for long walks, spend hours fishing, writing, listening, reading or working in the garden. Others of us see ourselves as having some kind of mission in life to improve or change the status quo. We may sit on committees, organize projects or become deeply involved in current affairs. Yet others of us see ourselves as being essentially 'family' or 'local' people, spending our time with our family or in group, club or team 'activities'.

With increased leisure time, identifying which one of these we are takes on a new importance. While we are in full-time employment, such questions can be put to one side but later we cannot hide behind a work-role when answering the question, 'What are you?' No longer are we a bus-conductor or secretary, a hairdresser or stockbroker. (It never was a complete answer anyway.)

There are many well-known contemporary personalities who have continued to enjoy useful and active lives well into their eighties and nineties. Among heads of state, President Tito is probably the most recent example, but many of us can remember General Charles de Gaulle, and some, our own

Winston Churchill, who returned to power as Prime Minister at the age of seventy-six. Gladstone was also remarkable, becoming Prime Minister for the fourth time at eighty-two. He carried all three readings of his Home Rule Bill, speaking on every amendment throughout its ninety-day duration. When he eventually 'retired' he completed several books including a translation of Horace. Churchill also finished his *History of the English Speaking Peoples* in his eighties. In a recent comment on the active life of some elder statesmen, A. L. Rowse also cites Harold Macmillan. Not long ago, at a celebration of Sir Arthur Bryant's eightieth birthday, much the best speech, he declared, was made by 86-year-old Harold Macmillan who then left the party to go off to China.

Titian continued to paint and accepted commissions throughout his nineties. His Piéta was left unfinished when he succumbed to the plague in his one hundredth year.

Of philosophers, Thomas Hobbes wrote his autobiography in Latin verse at eighty-four, and two years later finished his translation of the *Odyssey* and the *Iliad*. Bertrand Russell was active up to his death at ninety-seven and George Bernard Shaw up to ninety-four. Voltaire wrote his last story *The White Bull* at the age of eighty and four years later journeyed to Paris for the production of his last tragedy, *Irène*. Tennyson wrote *Crossing the Bar* when he was eighty and Robert Bridges had *The Testament of Beauty* published on his eighty-fifth birthday. His contemporary Dean Inge, gave the British Academy lecture on Origen at eighty-six and within the following two years published *The End of an Age* and *Mysticism in Religion*. He continued to write regular articles for newspapers until he was ninety-two which caused someone to enquire of him whether he was 'a pillar of the Church or two columns of the Evening Standard'.

In more recent times some of us have been privileged to listen to the spiced and original comments of 97-year-old commissioner Catherine Booth of the Salvation Army, and the succinct, lively and enthusiastic boat-race commentary of 75-year-old John Snagge. Karl Böhm, who died in 1981 in his mid-eighties, appeared to find a new vein of energy: although physical infirmity forced him to sit whilst conducting, it seemed to impair not a whit his control over the musicians. Writing in *The Daily Telegraph*, Alan Blyth commented:

In the Scherzo (of Dvorak's *New World Symphony*) Böhm travelled unerringly towards the Bohemian fields in which the music has its origins. Not a detail was overlooked by the conductor's wary eye as the work progressed in a spontaneous way wonderful to hear. On this form Böhm can defy the passing years.

Among other musicians, Pablo Casals continued to play the cello superbly and teach it, well into his eighties.

Even when 'retirement' is chosen, as in the case of Artur Rubinstein, his colourful mind, zest for life, humour, phenomenal memory and outrageous stories come tumbling out in published, two-volume autobiographical form, of which Blyth again writes:

> He lost nothing of his energy or enthusiasm until into his nineties, when his sight began to fail, nor – as these pages implicitly tell us – his generosity of heart and pocket. His sheer application and his enjoyment of life are an example to a later generation.

Rubinstein himself says 'Now I can't play I'm the happiest person in the world . . . I've never been as happy as now . . . it was getting boring listening to myself and I am enjoying having the time to listen to others.' He has found new ways of being himself.

University professors, broadcasters, artists, sportsmen, the latter including the single-handed round-the-world yachtsman Sir Francis Chichester, come to mind by the score. Certainly nothing terrible suddenly happened to *them* when they reached their sixtieth or sixty-fifth birthday. Indeed, in many instances, mind, body and soul appear to grow and develop. How can we help ourselves in similar fashion? How may we continue to develop our own mind, body and spirit? Let us consider each in turn, and first, the mind and further education.

Education
Education has many meanings; it includes important learning obtained informally by reading, by observation and by sheer experience. Education as a systematic process, involving

teaching as an aid to that learning, usually results in the acquisiton of knowledge and/or a skill.

Sidney Jones, the head of the School of Education at the Polytechnic of North London states that in terms of education, the second half of life may be conceived of as having three phases, the boundaries of which may act as indicators, for they are *not* precisely fixed. These, he suggests, are:

i) the pre-retirement phase;
ii) the central phase;
iii) the culmination phase.

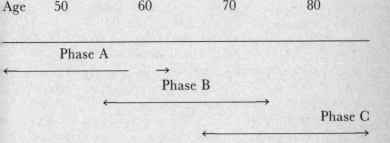

| Age | 50 | 60 | 70 | 80 |

'Phase A' includes the final years in regular employment. The substance of education in this period rests on preparation for retirement, or for a new career, or both. 'Phase B', the years following retirement, can constitute a leisure activity in its own right, as in the enjoyment of art or literature classes. It provides for the acquisition of skills on which a leisure activity can be built, such as gardening or golf. It is also an obvious ingredient in preparing for a new occupation which demands additional knowledge or skill. 'Phase C' for many people, is the period of increasing vulnerability to frailness and to disability. Education at this stage can contribute to the quality of life by providing enjoyable occupational preparation for this by the growth of knowledge and skill.

In the first phase, preparation for retirement is sometimes given by industrial, commercial and governmental organizations. Employees approaching retirement have the opportunity, in working hours, to attend a series of lectures or discussions. Programmes are conducted either on the firm's premises or at the local further education college. They are usually somewhat limited in scope and in length. A typical 'package' would be of six half-days' duration and include consideration of finance and taxation, looking after one's health and taking up new interests and hobbies. While useful, these programmes reach only a minority of employees, although the pre-Retirement Association is doing a good deal to propagate their value and to assist in their establishment. Pre-retirement courses run for members of HM Services are wider in scope and longer in duration. They can include such subjects as house-maintenance, upholstery and carpentry.

It is interesting that it is 'Phase C', the culminating phase, which has seen particular development of specifically designed educational ventures. This is mainly because the inactivity of long-stay patients in geriatric wards and residents in homes has shown up an obvious need. The introduction of this educational activity in institutions has wide and significant implications: it involves progressive and cumulative learning and systematic teaching; it has as goals the achievement of growing ability and mastery, and activities are no longer seen as mere occupations or pastimes.

It may be interesting for those who are responsible for the running of institutes for older people to know of some of the more outstanding examples quoted by Sidney Jones. The pioneering work of Sylvia Poulden in setting up art and craft classes in geriatric hospitals in London has resulted, it is reported, in her patients acquiring a new confidence, the ability to concentrate and an improvement in the standard of their work. In other words, they learnt. The work of Elizabeth Harwood in teaching singing to old people in Queensland, Australia, is also noteworthy. She called it a 'reactivation' programme. It led to the unaccustomed exercise of little-used muscles and an improvement in speaking voices. The patients, it is claimed, were led to a stronger sense of identification with their own pasts through the choice of songs and they also developed a new initiative.

Naylor and Harwood (again in Australia), have taught recorder playing to elderly people. This has resulted in better control of breathing and concentration, improved memory, better co-ordination between sight and muscles and a sense of rhythm as well as a sense of group responsibility and achievement.

Juliette Alvin has also described the therapeutic effects of her music programme in a geriatric department. The outcome, she has noted, includes a feeling of belonging, being wanted and a sense of achievement. These patients were said to have developed brighter eyes, better posture and, most important, experienced satisfaction and happiness.

Basil Berridge, a lecturer in further education, has been instrumental in initiating classes in pottery, yoga, art and music in North Hertfordshire's geriatric hospitals. They have, it is reported, 'met needs for stimulation and relaxation and provided an outlet for aggression. They have induced the exercise of disused muscles and given depressed patients an interest.'

Jean Mulford (also in further education), has instituted classes in Merseyside. She finds that the personal appearance, alertness and memory of her patients have improved, as have their sense of purpose and social behaviour. A particularly interesting finding, borne out in other hospitals, is that continence has improved as a concomitant of the educational programmes.

There are many other experiments and new programmes in hospitals and homes throughout the country. Sidney Jones himself has been associated with classes in poetry and play reading, in craft and current affairs at Northwick Park Hospital, and in art at the Hammersmith Hospital in London.

The number of old people in homes and hospitals however, whilst large, represents a small proportion of those people who are in the second half of their lives. More programmes are required for people outside institutions. In this country adult education is largely the responsibility of:

University extra-mural departments;
the Workers' Educational Association.
local authority adult education institutes;
residential colleges (mostly for weekends and longer periods at out-of-term times);
mutual, co-operative learning ventures (usually having a specialized purpose);
the Open University.

Most opportunity at the present time is offered in the broad category of 'liberal' studies: the arts, crafts, literature, music and philosophy, together with 'practical' activities such as dramatic production, gardening and house-decoration.

In education, the appetite grows by what it feeds on. The number of older people enrolling for further education is increasing and therefore the standards of education among members of our older population are also steadily increasing. By the year 2,000 the demand for higher education may well be very great indeed. To meet it, Jones believes that the only practical answer is open access to the higher education system, principally the universities and polytechnics but also the newly-developed institutes and colleges of higher education.

A sign of what is possible was given by the Committee of Directors of Polytechnics in the Autumn of 1978 in its response to the DHSS discussion document 'A Happier Old Age'. This spoke of polytechnics having:

> . . . the potential to contribute to the life of elderly people by opening access to their existing courses and programmes on a wide scale; providing programmes specially devised for older people in areas of special interest and concern; providing introductory programmes for those who may not otherwise feel able to enter higher education institutions directly, and setting up special centres which would co-ordinate and channel the existing and planned provision for elderly people.

Hatfield Polytechnic already has a scheme of open access for older people to degree courses in the humanities, while the Polytechnic of North London is considering the adoption of a scheme of widespread access by middle-aged and older persons to degree and other courses. The Open University, among its thousands of mature students in 1978, had four and a half thousand registered students between the ages of fifty-three and sixty-two and nearly one and a half thousand who were sixty-three or over. The Extra-Mural Department of the University of London conducted its first summer school for retired people in 1980, while the BBC offers a wide range of courses combining radio and television teaching with written publications.

For those who prefer 'a little learning' in pleasant surroundings, Embassy Hotels offer Leisure Learning weekends. These range from a weekend studying antiques in Yorkshire to a weekend based on various aspects of photography in the Cotswolds. Altogether there were eleven options and a choice of fifty-three weekends between October 1980 and September 1981. The fee includes two nights' accommodation, all meals, lectures and guides. Music weekends are run by Trust House Forte Ltd, and again fees include accommodation and meals.

as well as the concerts. Brochures are available from the main office of each of these hotel chains.

The Open University's 'Guide for Applicants' contains useful addresses of outside agencies, regional offices of the Open University and a nation-wide list of study centres.

Recreation

For some people, education will also be recreation, but others will enjoy the extra time which can be devoted to already established hobbies and to developing new interests. The local library or town hall should have addresses of tennis courts, swimming baths, golf courses, bowling greens, squash courts, photography, drama and play-reading groups etc. If there is difficulty, the local Age Concern branch or Citizens Advice Bureau may be able to help. To solve transport problems, it is worth contacting the Age Concern group in the locality; several of them run transport schemes for elderly people in need.

Women may welcome the opportunity of spending more time in home-making and enjoy learning Cordon Bleu or Escoffier cookery, upholstery or dress-making. In the country there is much free food to be gathered, cooked or stored. Mushrooms, blackberries, sloes, rose-hips (for syrup), dandelion leaves (for salads), crab apples, Japonica fruits (they add an extra something to marmalade) and sweet chestnuts are but a few, and there are useful paper backs on 'free food' obtainable from booksellers. Advantage can be taken of the pick-it-yourself schemes operated by many farmers and market gardeners; potatoes, vegetables and soft fruit are usually good buys, and a year's supply of jams and chutneys can bring a warming sense of achievement as well as a pleasant saving of money. There will also be time to experiment with new dishes, to arrange flowers, to dry leaves for winter decoration, to make one's own furniture polish, to preserve vegetables (our ancestors did survive without deep freezers), bottle fruit and make presents or Christmas and birthday cards from paintings, sketches or holiday snaps. The list is never-ending; which hobbies are chosen depends upon interest, talent, location, resources and circumstances. But in the words of Disraeli, 'Increased means and increased leisure are the two civilizers of man.' Even if only one is increased the prospect to learn something new can still be exciting.

The Sundial Society offers 'cultural pursuits and social contacts' for elderly people, and for those who wish to organize a stage production Age Concern have published a guide 'On Stage for the Over 60s'.

Other organizations offer amenities (for example, wireless sets) or facilitate sports (for example, angling) or hobbies (for example, amateur wireless) for handicapped people. Names and addresses are given in the Appendix.

Housebound elderly people who would like the stimulation of a visitor from time to time should contact the local Age Concern group, the local church, Red Cross, branch of St John Ambulance, St Andrew's (Scotland) or Contact.

Work
Many of these local groups or branches of national organizations, have, among their volunteers, people who themselves are retired from paid employment. Participants at a recent Age Concern seminar recommended that more attempts could be made by voluntary and community groups to *involve* elderly people in their activities, not just to *provide for* them. Professionals and volunteers often seem to deny elderly people the simple joy of giving (an act that is often known to be more satisfying than that of receiving), while of course practising it themselves. Certainly, continuing to work, albeit in a voluntary capacity, can be a stimulating activity for both mind and body.

For those who are able to get about, there are several Age Concern schemes in which to participate. A street warden scheme, for example, can give interest and is certainly worth-while work. The idea behind such a scheme might be to:

  keep a watchful and unobtrusive eye on elderly people in the area;

  keep an eye on elderly people who are 'at risk' for one reason or another;

  arrange daily or regular calls to check on one person's well-being;

  keep an eye on all people 'at risk' (of whatever age) who have said they would like to participate in the scheme;

provide help on an emergency or 'one-off' basis.

The Age Concern 'Action Guide: Street Warden Schemes' provides a single step-by-step guide for people who would like to initiate such a scheme in their own area. It is written for people who have not previously been involved in similar work, but who feel it might help to meet the needs in their local community. There are also 'Hospital After Care Schemes' operated by some Age Concern groups, which aim to meet some of the needs of elderly people discharged from hospital. For those who have 'green fingers' or are 'good-about-the-house', there are 'Practical Help Schemes' which enable volunteers to provide assistance in such tasks as shopping, travelling, gardening, cooking, cleaning or decorating on a long-term, short-term or a 'one-off' basis. Many large Age Concern branches would welcome volunteers to enlarge their ranks.

For those who seek paid employment, there are several organizations who aim to put older people in touch with suitable jobs. Success After Sixty deals mostly with office staff and the Over Sixties Employment Bureaux will advise on prospects in other fields also. The Over-Forty Association for Women Workers gives employment advice as well as information and help on housing. The Pre-Retirement Association, publish *Choice Magazine*, incorporating 'Life Begins at 50'. (They also publish two useful books *Money and your Retirement* and *In the Pink: a Health Guide*). It is worth remembering, however, that before taking up paid employment, advice should always be sought on questions of income tax, pensions and national insurance contributions.

Perhaps one of the most valuable forms of 'work' older people can do is to share their experience. In drawing together some of the major points raised during discussions at an Age Concern seminar, Niall Dickson observed, 'It is the height of irony that we have to ask ourselves "What can they offer?" when we are referring to the most experienced members of our society. Present trends indicate the potential benefit both to the elderly and the rest of the community. There are now tenants' associations which actively encourage retired people to become involved and help run their affairs and there are schools which recognize the value of elderly people as "live" history lessons.'

The same principle applies to leisure pursuits. An elderly

member of a fishing club or a wine society, carpentry or cooking class can pass on expertise to younger members.

Love and 'Things of the Spirit'

Loving and being loved do not stop when one reaches a certain birthday: they may, as suggested earlier, be expressed in different ways. Some older people continue to have intercourse at a considerable age. For the majority, however, companionship without passion may develop, and once more the couple will find 'new ways of being themselves' in love.

Possibly the most neglected area (by those who have contact with old people) and one which offers opportunities for development and help for younger persons, is that of the spirit. Personal beliefs, hopes, aspirations and philosophies of life develop over the years and often crystallize in later ones. There are signs that western culture is now including a rather more intelligent interest in things spiritual and some churches have ceased playing down their spiritual role in an effort to keep up with the times. Whether, and when, we as individuals do so will be a personal and private development, but many older people find with Wordsworth that not only do they just continue to be but that they become 'greater than they know. . .'

Appearance and the Body

Certainly good grooming becomes even more important as we age. Unkempt hair, finger-nails, spotted clothing and laddered stockings are unattractive at any age: in older people they are even more accentuated because of sagging muscles, skin and, in some instances, stance. Effort has to be made to stand upright and as straight-backed as Victorians but it could be achieved more often than it is. Good health and physical exercise can help. For those interested in physical fitness and beauty-through-health, the Keep-Fit Association and the Women's League of Health and Beauty will supply addresses of local teachers and classes, as well as leaflets describing home-exercises.

The sparser hair of old age requires greater attention than the thicker hair of youth. This generation has the advantage of thickening conditioners and rinses to help them. A good cut can help considerably and cheaper rates are available for pensioners in some hairdressers. Even if one is not going anywhere, one's own morale is uplifted by knowing one looks good and all efforts should be made to achieve that aim.

For many women, professional facial massages and packs are out of the question, but just remembering to apply and remove cleansing cream and astringent lotion with upward strokes will help a little to counter-balance those drooping face muscles. The neck can also be given 'food' in the form of moisturiser. While proprietary cosmetics are expensive, now more time is available, face packs, all-purpose cleansing creams and astringent lotions can be made at home from ingredients stocked by most chemists. For example:

An All-Purpose Cold Cream

> 1oz beeswax
> 7oz (200 mls) liquid paraffin
> $^1/_3$ teaspoonful borax
> ¾ pint boiling water

> Melt beeswax in liquid paraffin in a basin standing in boiling water. This takes about ten minutes and need not be watched. When beeswax is melted, remove from the heat. Add borax to boiling water and add these to the wax mix. Stir and pour into jars. Leave to cool.

Skin Tonic (not astringent, so good for ageing, dry skin)

> 1 tablespoonful glycerine
> 1 tablespoonful witch-hazel
> 2 tumblersful distilled water

> Mix all ingredients and add a few drops of triple rose water for a pleasant smell and a slight colour. For oily skins, add a little more witch-hazel.

Baths

Baths can be made invigorating and sweet smelling by adding a few rosemary and bay leaves (tied in a small muslin bag). For a flowery scent, dry flower petals, especially rose petals and lavender, can be tied into a small muslin bag and hung under the hot water tap of the bath.

Toilet Soap

The remains of tablets of soap can be melted in an old saucepan with a little glycerine and while still warm, moulded into balls for further use. The beauty editors of some women's magazines will supply other recipes, and many old housekeeping books also contain excellent ones.

Care of the Skin, Nails and Hair

The skin of the body becomes dry as well as thinner in age; this can be alleviated to some extent by applying baby lotion or cream. (Bath oils can be dangerous as they cause the bath to become slippery: some also make it difficult to clean the bath.) Nails may become dry and brittle but a little cream massaged into their base at night will often strengthen them. Toe-nails should be regularly attended to, as they can quickly become hard, horny and ingrowing, and in time may even make walking difficult and painful.

Make-up may need to be changed. The skin is thinner so foundation cream or liquid may also need to be of a thinner consistency than before. Rouge colouring will require handling with extra care: a little goes a long way and must be subtly blended. The same goes for eye make-up: this is even more difficult to apply if spectacles are needed in order to see properly: the advice of a *good* friend may be helpful in order to determine the amount and colour now suitable.

Tiny lines sometimes form around the mouth so it may be necessary to change to a less oily lipstick, as drier ones do not run into small 'rivulets' around the lips. Warmer-coloured and lighter-textured face powder will probably be more flattering, again because of changing skin cells. For those who have scars or ageing blemishes they wish to hide, the British Red Cross Society and the Society of Skin Camouflage will give useful information.

Hair colouring is a matter of personal preference, but most women who have tinted hair like to use lighter tones gradually, until the time to go natural is reached. The darker, harsher tones tend to look artificial later in life, even if they did not do so in middle age.

Clothing

The lighter, subtle colours are usually preferable in clothes also. Most women know the trick of wearing white near the face: the reflected light effect is flattering at any age. This principle of light colours enhancing one's appearance holds good for most people when older. Even those who have been unable to wear camel or oatmeal colours during their earlier years may find that they can in old age. Similarly, although it appears paradoxical, black becomes more flattering for some older people who have been unable to wear it before.

Clothes are very expensive and their good care has become even more vital in recent years. A good dry-cleaner is sometimes hard to find but it is well worth paying a little extra rather than having one's clothes ruined at a cheaper price. There are also some excellent 'spot-removers' on the market (Goddards is especially effective). Well-pressed clothes, even if they are older than one would wish, will enhance appearance and morale. But perhaps the greatest beautifiers of all, at any age, are happiness and good health. Let us now consider how to promote and maintain the latter.

CHAPTER 7

KEEPING FIT AND WELL

I want death to find me planting cabbages, caring little for it and much more for my imperfect garden.

Montaigne 1533–1592

To keep fit and well is an aim of most of us throughout life and it is important for our old age that it should be. Fresh air, adequate exercise, a balanced diet and sufficient fluids are all important in achieving that independence we wish to attain throughout our life-span. Yet many of us pay less attention to our own body than we do to our motor-cars.

We know that physical and mental dependence are usually related to physical and mental incapacities. One can be totally dependent upon others through illness at any age. The lesson to be learned is the importance of the prevention of illness and injury.

With ageing, we run an increased risk of accidents, whether they be burns, cuts, traffic accidents or falls. The amount of stimulation, such as heat or pain, required to provoke signals of the sensory nerve endings increases and the speed of transmission within the nerve fibres slows down, hence the weak and slow responses of nerves to external and internal stimuli. It has been demonstrated, however, that the speed with which nerves conduct stimuli can be increased by training. While it remains difficult for an individual to train his own reflexes, this research has value inasmuch as it has demonstrated that 'growing old' can be postponed by regular activity or training.

For example, there are few people whose arterial walls (the walls of the largest blood vessels in our bodies) remain smooth and resilient by the time they reach seventy. While such changes may be considered to be caused by disease, they do increase with age. In an advanced state, such a condition of our blood vessels can cause a shortage of blood supply to our vital organs and the functioning of these will be impaired, or even stopped: hardening of these blood vessels is one of the leading causes of death in many countries of the world. Yet we know of ways to prevent the *progression* of this condition: ways which are all the more effective if maintained from childhood onwards. For this reason, warnings of the presence of malfunctioning or disease should be acted upon at once. Some people recommend regular 'screening' in order to pick up such warnings at an early stage.

Again, the loss of elastic fibres of the lung decreases the body's vital capacity. Sometimes the thin walls of the air sacs diminish and merge. This results in a reduced surface area for the exchange of atmospheric gases, a condition called emphysema. Cigarette smoke, atmospheric pollutants (diesel fumes, aerosols etc.) as well as bacterial and viral infections can all cause bronchitis, and both these respiratory conditions lessen the efficient functioning of the lungs. While this impairment sometimes goes un-noticed when the body does not put a high demand on the lungs, it becomes noticeable when extra demand is made, when, for example, one runs upstairs or after a moving bus. Eventually the 'margin of safety' becomes slim and the older the person the more serious the consequences, until even minor respiratory infections cause serious illnesses and sometimes even death.

In young people, physical and intellectual standards can be determined broadly speaking, according to age, and these standards can be applied to a given population. Older people, on the other hand, vary widely. After suffering from bleeding of the brain (cerebral haemorrhage) or a stroke, a man or woman of forty or fifty may be bedridden and speechless. A man of eighty, on the other hand, may be a vigorous prime-minister of his country. Attempts are currently being made to compute indices for biological ageing which will serve as a more reliable guide than chronological age. It has been found difficult during this work, however, to draw a distinction between the form of reference for pathology (disease) and that for the normal ageing process. This is because diseases such as those we have just considered – emphysema, chronic bronchitis and strokes – play a major part in determining the life-style one adopts as well as one's life expectancy. Yet to a large extent it is possible for us ourselves to prevent such diseases and thereby reduce the likelihood of that dreaded state of 'being a nuisance to others'.

We now recognize that man, as a biological species, can live as long as ninety or even a hundred and ten years. But health hazards are of two kinds, biological and social. Many of the health problems that diminish the quality of life beyond the age of sixty are due to self-inflicted damage in earlier decades; damage caused by over-eating, over-drinking, over-smoking, over-stress and under-exercise. Variations of this statement have been made many times in many places from many platforms, and in almost all literature on ageing. Yet, as a warning, it is ignored. Because it is ignored, there is likely to be in this country, in the future, a large number of over sixty-year-olds who will have few years of good *quality* living. This is well illustrated by Carruthers in his book *The Western Way of Death*.

Personal health has a number of different facets which, together with adaptation to the circumstances in which one leads one's life, are important at any age. Hoyman has considered them thus:

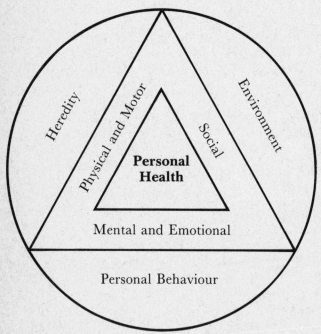

Figure II Facets of Personal Health and Its Three Foundations

Health Promotion

MacDonald-Wallace, senior lecturer at the West London Institute of Higher Education, suggests:

The physical and motor aspects of health are readily recognized. Any aches and pains, malfunction of one system
or another, or difficulty in movement or skill–performance
usually sends one scurrying for help to one's medical
adviser. The social aspects are not taken so seriously. The
fact that a man does not get on with his colleagues, has
frequent rows with his wife or family, and relates poorly to
other people in his environment is just as likely to be the
cause of the onset of physical illness as is the latter to be
the case of unsocial behaviour.

Nor can we usually isolate mental and emotional disturbance from the other aspects. There is inevitable interaction, in which mental or emotional maladjustment may
lead to emotional and physical troubles, and, of course,
physical or motor malfunction may lead to social, mental
and emotional imbalance which is a loss of that integrity
which is health.

Taking the three 'foundations' first, there is no doubt that
heredity plays a large part in our health. Genetic defects, not
always known, mean that life is harder for some than others.
That does not mean that genetic defects cannot be overcome
for there are plenty of examples to prove otherwise. Neither
does it mean that the *quality* of life need be less because of
congenital or inherited defect. Again, many individuals have
proven otherwise. But health is *affected* by heredity.

Likewise, the environment into which we are born is important. A happy, stable family life, adequate food, housing,
warmth, clothing and stimuli for emotional and intellectual
development will influence our future lives, including our
health.

The third foundation which Hoyman calls the 'major pillar
of wisdom in matters of health', is one's own personal behaviour. One can ensure that one's personal behaviour is not
maladaptive nor destructive of the quality of life in later years
by a little self-understanding, some knowledge and the acquisition of a few skills.

Health Education Courses
Practically every book written on the care of the elderly includes discussion of problems arising from poor nutrition,

inefficient heart and blood vessels, obesity, 'bad feet', lack of psychological stimuli and loneliness.

Several attempts have been made up and down the country to meet the needs of people who require appropriate knowledge and relevant skills to help them with these problems. In one instance, after a course of six talks on health education, it was concluded by the course director that, 'the average elderly person will learn nothing new unless it can be proved that the knowledge to be acquired is vital to his or her wellbeing'. Individuals and organizations who aim to meet these particular needs of the elderly population, would do well to bear this finding in mind.

In the medical field, the work of Maddison in Middlesex and that of Ferguson Anderson and his colleagues in Glasgow are good examples of how the quality of living can be improved and maintained in old age. The Maddison Clinic has now spawned others and the age range of attenders is something like fifty-five to ninety with the groups coming from varying social strata. As well as being diagnostic centres, the clinics have advisory and counselling functions. Subjects about which advice has been sought range from posture, diet and exercise to laws on tenancy or where to borrow a wheelchair. The work involves representatives of many of those disciplines and professions referred to earlier: health educators, dentists, opticians, chiropodists, physiotherapists, social workers and health visitors, as well as doctors and nurses. Often the secretarial staff and receptionists are in close touch with the communities from which the people come. Several such clinics up and down the country have reported remarkable physical and personality changes over the years. Such centres, operating as a source of expectancy and inspiration for those determined to get the most out of their later years, have also become social centres for those in need of company and stimulation.

Other health education ventures for the elderly have been reported from time to time, but unfortunately not all towns and cities have them. Some health courses last for a month or so, involving a few hours attendance each week. Students look at their own physical problems, are encouraged to make decisions about seeking dental and medical treatment, learn about *proper* hearing-aids and *suitable* spectacles and are taught how to keep their feet in good condition. They learn simple facts about essential foods, are shown useful and effective exercises they can perform at home, and discuss inter-personal relationships. The latter is a subject in which, it is reported, many elderly people are intensely interested.

Exercise helps to maintain mobility of various joints, from fingers to toes, knees to neck, and it also helps to lessen the diminishing density of bones which leads to brittleness. Since exercise helps to keep the heart and lungs in better condition, it also ensures a supply of oxygen to all cells of the body and in particular to those cells of the brain which are essential for mental as well as physical activity. It can keep the muscles of the stomach (abdomen) stronger, strengthen the muscles of the back and legs and can also help to prevent the development of varicose veins and ulcers. It can give a psychological uplift and help to keep one's feet active and strong.

Healthy feet are often taken for granted but when in poor condition can produce postural changes that bring aches and pains to various parts of the body. They also slow down movement which can lead to increasing weakness of the heart, the circulation of blood and can also increase the risk of obesity. The latter in turn further restricts movements. Chiropodists are in short supply throughout the country, so clearly prevention is better than being at the end of very long waiting lists.

Information about such courses as those described here can be obtained from the nearest district health authority (address in the telephone book) or from the Health Education Council in London or from a local institute or centre of higher (or adult) education.

Diet in Old Age

If diet is wrong the chances of developing heart and circulatory diseases (thrombosis and hardening of the arteries) and nervous diseases increase.

Obtaining Food

Fresh food, well prepared and in balanced proportions will give one an adequate diet at any age. Unfortunately, in old age one or more of these factors is frequently missing. If one lives far from the shops and has no refrigerator, food storage can become a problem. With the closure of so many village or 'corner' shops, many old people find that they have to rely upon the large supermarkets in towns, most of which will not deliver. This is where friends or neighbours or a member from one of the voluntary organizations can help. Whilst it is important for elderly people to be active and independent, it is asking a lot to expect an 80-year-old to carry baskets of food up and down the steps of buses or for some distance on foot. There are, of course, baskets on wheels which are invaluable for short walking distances.

In Scandinavia, groups of elderly people are ensuring that they get very fresh food daily. They have created 'colonies' (of varying social and economic classes) just outside large towns or cities. There they are developing gardens, orchards, market gardens and small dairies in order to produce a good deal of their own food through a kind of producer/consumer type programme. Some home-grown fruit and vegetables are deep frozen while others are stored for all-year use. On some 'estates' a few cows are kept, and fresh butter, cheese and yoghurt as well as milk and cream, are produced for all. Such work and self-sufficiency is not without attraction even at an earlier age.

Food and drink are, of course, expensive items for all of us these days. However, unless contra-indicated by a physical condition or disease, a well-balanced diet of protein (fish or meat), cheese, milk and eggs, with plenty of vegetables, fruit and an adequate intake of other roughage, such as granary or wholemeal bread or bran, is best.

Unfortunately, many old people, especially if living alone, give up bothering about food and just keep pangs of hunger at bay by eating bread, cake and biscuits (often all made from refined flour) and drinking tea with sugar and milk. Together with little or no exercise, this kind of diet quickly results in weight gain and very often, constipation. The latter condition in turn can lead to local disorders, such as piles or varicose veins or to a generalized illness resulting in an acute effect on brain activity.

Taking Food

The appetites of elderly people sometimes need to be stimulated and the taking of an aperitif or a glass of wine with the meal is to be recommended unless this is contra indicated on medical grounds. It can be said that wine is expensive, but old age does not, or should not, mean pauperism. The encouragement of individual enjoyments is vital and can be an important contribution of family members. Unfortunately, even presents for elderly relatives have become stereotyped and we are inclined to give lavender water, talcum powder, a box of handkerchiefs or a tin of biscuits, even for Christmas and birthdays. Why not a bottle of wine, or Scotch?

One of the most frequent causes of inadequate food intake amongst old people is ill-fitting dentures. The shape of the mouth and gums changes over the years and dentures also need to be changed accordingly. Regular visits to the dentist are just as important in old age as they are at any other stage of life, regardless of whether one is dentulous or not.

If special diets are required, for example diabetic, financial help may sometimes be needed, in which case the old person's general practitioner, district nurse or health visitor will be able to advise. The British Diabetic Association will also give useful information.

Cooking Food

Cooking food is sometimes difficult: certainly cooking an appetizing meal for just oneself presents problems for most of us at any age. One is often tempted to eat convenience foods, or to nibble little and often. Old people living alone need encouragement to prepare a good meal for themselves; this can be given in the form of one of the paperback publications on the subject of cooking for one or two people. Some of these books contain recipes for nutritious, cheap and easily-prepared dishes.

If a physical disability, such as osteo-arthritis of the hands, is the problem, there are many kitchen aids and adaptations for easier preparation and cooking of food. The Disabled Living Foundation and other Aids Centres have a wide variety of practical suggestions and of equipment on display and are ready and happy to discuss individual needs and difficulties from a professional viewpoint. They will also send information lists and answer individual queries by post from both elderly people and their professional advisors. A full assessment may be necessary to identify the most suitable aid in specific circumstances for a particular individual. The domiciliary occupational therapist or, in their absence, Social Services Departments will also be able to advise and should be contacted through the general practitioner or the local authority.

Available Services

If the old person still finds getting meals very difficult, the meals-on-wheels service (requested through the GP, health visitor, social worker or district nursing sister) will do the best it can. Unfortunately, in many areas the service is over extended and under staffed and can provide only one or two hot meals a week. Some social services departments pay neighbours of old people to cook at weekends for them. But eating *with* someone is for what most isolated old people long, and company can also stimulate the appetite. If possible, cooking for each other, taking it in turns to provide either the first course or the pudding, provides some interest. Alternatively, in many districts there are luncheon clubs and the local social services department or branch of Age Concern should know the address.

Some families have 'adopted' one elderly person living nearby and provide meals over a long period. These need not be 'given': he or she often prefers to pay a small sum for it and so maintain a degree of independence. This home-cooking is usually preferred to the mass cooking which is 'never quite the same', and one certainly does not develop a taste for the latter just because one has reached a certain age. The 'adopted' grandmamma or grandpapa can in turn give to the 'adopters' and their children, in the form of company, experience, memories, wisdom or interest, or sometimes more material gifts such as flowers from the garden or small treasures from the past, just as many grandparents have done over the generations. The pleasure and luxury of giving should not be denied them.

Another alternative can be provided as an individualized service by local volunteers. The local Voluntary Workers Bureau may be able to provide a volunteer to shop, prepare and cook a meal every so often. Some members of the Red Cross, St John Ambulance and (in Scotland) St Andrew's are able not only to prepare a meal but also to see that the old person is comfortable before giving it to him. He may need to have his dentures or glasses cleaned, be helped into an upright position, be taken to the w.c. or to wash his hands. The well-prepared volunteer should be able to meet all these needs as well as helping with the actual taking of the food and fluids if necessary. These volunteers are members of the public living in the neighbourhood who have taken courses of training in auxiliary nursing and social work in their spare time and have passed an examination to ensure a good level of competency and efficiency. They are also appreciative of the importance of confidentiality in any work they undertake, or any information they may acquire, during the carrying out of their unpaid duties. The addresses of local branches of these organizations will be in the local telephone directory.

Taking Exercise

Taking exercise should be, like everything else, done in moderation, and as a life-long habit. 'If I'd known I was gonna last this long', said W. C. Fields, 'I would've taken better care of myself.' Better care in the form of regular exercise usually begins in extreme youth but with increasing age and the pre-occupations of work and career, family and business in the middle years, many of us take less and less. The motor-car positively encourages us to do so. Little wonder then that our muscles get slacker than they need and our heart and lungs make themselves heard when we sprint for a moving bus, and that we put on weight.

A reasonable amount of walking, twenty to thirty minutes or so a day, is a good habit to have and a gradual increase in the time spent can be built up over a period of months. Such a routine has been found even more important after retirement when most people use up less energy, but continue to eat and drink the same amounts.

Some local health authorities have set up keep-fit classes or gymnasiums, while many councils offer special rates to older people who wish to use their swimming baths, tennis courts or bowling facilities. Information on these can be obtained at the local town hall. It is wise to check with one's GP before beginning any new form of exercise.

When specific remedial exercises are required, a domiciliary physiotherapist may visit but general information on routine keep-fit exercises should be forthcoming from the GP or the health visitor in the primary care team.

Keeping Mentally Healthy and Combatting Loneliness

Writing for the Folio Society, Sue Bradbury has declared:

> To be told that one's chances of living to be over eighty
> are greatly improved is, in my view, only encouraging if
> one can be sure of being physically capable of ski-ing and
> mentally capable of using one's leisure to tackle Proust.
> . . . One great aunt of my acquaintance goes off annually
> to do one, and another, while drawing a line at the original
> French, is wrestling with *Within a Budding Grove* . . . A
> combination of these two aunts is what I should like to be
> when I grow old.

Most of us would have similar wishes to be alert and interesting as well as physically fit. 'Activity' in old age does not
only mean work, any more than it should at any age. Study,
either individually or in groups, is attractive and activates
those failing brain cells. The advantage of group study is, as
one octogenarian said recently, 'that it gets one out of the
house'. There is also, of course, the Open University for those
who have the discipline to study alone.

Voluntary work is also available in many areas. The Voluntary Workers Bureaux up and down the country try to
match the volunteer to the job. The variety of work they offer
may include: cataloguing for a museum; envelope-addressing
for a charity or art gallery; account-keeping for a voluntary
organization; translating for a museum; helping with a local
arts festival; custodial care in an art gallery; programme selling for local concerts and theatres; helping with meals-on-
wheels or the warden of an old people's home or at a
luncheon-club; gardening or shopping; cooking or taking the
dog for a walk for someone who is ill or disabled. The choice
can be great and therefore volunteers with a variety of skills
and knowledge are required.

It is important that it is work which *needs* to be done and
not just something specially created, 'to keep the old boy
occupied'. One wants to know that it is important to get up
in the morning and that someone is relying upon you doing
so. For those interested in international work, recent activities
of Help the Aged provide several opportunities.

Membership or associateships of organizations also bring
regular interest, even by post. Local play-reading, drama
groups, concerts, and choirs, as well as local politics all have

a place. Theatre, opera and ballet tickets are less expensive outside London, but some theatres in the metropolis offer special rates at some performances. Mobile libraries visit many villages and towns now but others often have volunteers who will exchange books for housebound readers. It is worth enquiring.

A growing lack of mobility can, of course, narrow one's sphere of contact with the outside world, and may lead, if allowed to do so, to isolation and loneliness. The degree of loneliness felt usually depends upon the lifestyle that the old person and his family have lived in the past. It also depends upon individual personality. People who are gregarious and have always enjoyed the companionship of others will continue to do so in later life, while those who have never led such a life are unlikely to do so in old age. To some people, being alone is a desirable necessity and isolation does not inevitably mean loneliness. But for those for whom it does, the effect can be devastating. It is often caused by feelings of deprivation, helplessness and low self-esteem, leading to that deadliness of enemies, self-pity. So visitors and companions become even fewer and the condition is exacerbated.

Interest in others of all ages, work, study, recreation, physical exercise, mental explorations of new ideas, keeping a finger on happenings, local, national and international, can be beneficial. Some deterioration, however, is often inevitable and this is when one's attitude towards the ageing process is so very important, because it will play a prominent part in how we cope with the changes it brings.

Keeping Warm

Warmth is also vital for health in old age. In a recent national survey conducted among over-65-year-olds living in their own homes, it was found that 10 per cent had abnormally low core temperatures (or were suffering a degree of hypothermia).

Anyone can suffer from hypothermia at any age. Very young babies are also particularly vulnerable because their temperature-regulating centres are not fully developed. Sportsmen and women, sailors, mountaineers and walkers are the other group most often associated with the condition. It is, however, most common in old people.

Usually when one's body temperature falls, the thermostat or temperature-control centre in the brain goes into action and increases heat production by releasing hormones to create energy and reduces heat loss by cutting down on the blood supply to the skin, hands and feet. In old age, this centre is not always efficient, so although cold may be felt, one's brain and body do not respond to it. Some drugs and all alcohol predispose to hypothermia, so if an old person is taking a quantity of either, extra care should also be taken. Some old people do not even feel the cold and so will not take the appropriate action to warm themselves, such as putting on more clothes, drinking hot liquid, stepping up the heating system or by just walking about.

Clothes

Clothes play an important part in keeping warm and several layers of clothing are better than one thick one. Very heavy clothes are also more tiring to wear. They are also less effective than wearing, for example, a thinner top coat over a vest, petticoat, dress, cardigan and jacket. In the house, the same principle applies; cardigans, jackets, shawls or ponchos over the main garment will be warmer than one heavy suit. In very cold weather thick nightdresses or pyjamas should be worn in bed, while quilted bed-jackets, coat-linings and dressing gowns provide warm yet lightweight extras. Bedsocks and mittens are not to be scorned and our ancestors were wise to have night caps (the woolly kind). The amount of heat one loses from one's head is very high. Travelling rugs and duvets are preferred to heavy blankets by some people while flannelette sheets are warmer than cotton ones.

If sensible warm underwear is difficult to buy locally, some of the mail order firms are often able to supply it. One firm makes an excellent 'spacecoat' which is a housecoat made of insulated and fire-proof material. If financial help is needed for warm clothing, those people who receive supplementary pension may in some circumstances be able to claim a single payment.

Hot Drinks

All hot drinks as well as hot food help one to keep warm. Drinking the hot contents of a thermos flask just before switching off the light at night will stand one in good stead, whilst a hot drink in the middle of the night from another flask kept by the bedside will help to maintain heat until the morning. If it is found that this habit leads to incontinence at night, the timing should be suitably adjusted.

Heating Aids and Appliances

Hot water bottles are useful not only in bed. Well-covered, they can be 'nursed' all day long. If hands are arthritic or shaky those bottles which stand and do not need to be held for filling are safer than the rubber variety. If a rubber one is preferred, there are 'neck-holders' available which can usually be obtained through a domiciliary occupational therapist. Any local authority office Health Department or Aids Centre should be able to provide information. Hot water bottle covers should be used in all instances.

There are now many electric blankets which can be left on all night. These extra low voltage (ELV) blankets are safe even if wetted (for example, if the old person is incontinent of urine). Sometimes the social services department is able to lend one. If this is not possible and it is decided to buy one, the 'best buys' according to *Which* magazine (November 1977) are Dee Gee G5 or Halcyon CU3 (single-bed size) or Dee Gee SUB 24 or Safesleeper SL (double-bed size).

Heating the House

While all electrical appliances must be treated with due caution and their instructions carefully noted by people of all ages, because of the swaying motion which often accompanies the ageing process, fires do contain a special danger to old people and should always be guarded.

Heating one room and not the rest of the house can result in draughts, so in order to conserve the heat in any one room, heating the whole building must be considered. If there is an external wall, a gas convector heater is safe and economical. Insulation of the loft and hot and cold water tanks is another possibility. A grant is available from the local authority for insulation purposes (i.e. for 66 per cent of the cost up to £50). Elderly people receiving supplementary pensions, rent/rate rebates or rent allowances, and severely disabled people, can claim a grant of 90 per cent of the cost up to a maximum of £90. Further details are given in the leaflet 'Save Money on Loft Insulation' obtainable from Citizens Advice Bureaux and town halls. If just gaps around doors and windows need sealing and help is required to do this, it it worth contacting the local Age Concern group.

It should be remembered that neither an improvement grant nor a single payment can be claimed for wall insulation. If dampness of walls and ceiling is a problem, it should first be ascertained that this is not due to condensation from saucepans, kettles, gas heaters, cookers or calor gas fires. If none of these is the cause, the environmental health officer at the nearest local authority may be able to help.

The amount of heating needed to keep warm is a very individual requirement. For the majority of people, a room at a temperature of 21°C (70°F) is usually acceptable. The lowest room temperature should be 18°F (65°F). This applies to the corridors, stairs, hall, w.c., etc. as well as the usual 'living' room. When a cooler bedroom is preferred, the bed must be warm and arrangements made so that it remains so. If worried about the fall of temperature at night in an elderly person's room, a maximum/minimum thermometer will record both the highest and the lowest temperatures reached in a room and after taking these readings, the heating system can be adjusted accordingly.

Some old people can probably afford more than they actually spend on fuel or heating. They will still set aside the same sum of money for such items as they have done for years, because they have not adapted to the results of inflation. Others, brought up to be thrifty and save for a rainy day, do not recognize that the rainy day has arrived. Once again, friends and relatives can encourage them to enjoy their savings sensibly.

For those who do need help with meeting their fuel bills, there are some benefits which can be claimed. The local Citizens Advice Bureau should be contacted for details.

Walking About

We all know that 'keep moving' is good advice in cold weather but unfortunately mobility is not always a strong characteristic of old people. It must, however, be encouraged, even if one is taking a calculated risk of accidents. It may appear safer and easier for all concerned if the swaying old person is discouraged, but there are just as many medical hazards associated with inactivity. They include the risk of incontinence and the loss of other muscle tone, pressure sores (similar to bed-sores), the formation of blood clots (thromboses) and depression. There are other physiological considerations also. Lying or sitting about causes an appreciable loss of calcium from the bones which become fragile and more likely to break during a fall. Even very healthy astronauts on space flights are in danger of this during their long periods of comparative inactivity. This is another reason why moderate physical exercise *at all ages* is vital to our health and well-being.

The Right to Take Risks

It has to be remembered that if an elderly person wishes to remain in a cold house and risk hypothermia in spite of authoritative opinions and advice, he or she should be allowed to do so.

Making the Home as Safe as Possible

Many families, while wishing to preserve their elderly relative's independence, also wish to have peace of mind concerning their safety. Much can be done to prevent accidents and it is important to see that the old person's home contains as few hazards as possible. It has been found that the most frequent causes of old people falling in their homes are due to environmental factors: poor lighting, poor colour contrast, objects left lying on the floor, sliding rugs, polished linoleum and so on. Such hazards combined with the impaired balance mechanism can be lethal, literally.

Fire is probably the risk first thought of by both relatives and neighbours. The main causes of fires in this country are cigarettes, pipes and matches, and not heaters as most people believe. Cigarette lighters are safer than matches. Everyone should be discouraged from smoking in bed. The taking of drugs in the form of medicine or sedation and the consumption of alcohol heighten this danger at any age as each induces sleep, but because vision and the sense of smell may be diminished in old age, the risk is greater in older people. If the habit is unbreakable, some safeguard can be provided by seeing that bedclothes, night gowns, shirts and pyjamas are flame-resistant. Small fire extinguishers are comparatively cheap and a fire blanket should be kept in an accessible place.

If neighbours are anxious, they should be informed about where these items are to be found.

If the house has old wiring, the local electricity show-room or Citizens Advice Bureau should be contacted and advice sought. If it is decided that new wiring is needed, it may be possible to obtain a maturity loan from the local authority.

Any fireguard should be fixed to a wall. Diminishing vision can mean that certain hazards, such as the raised or frayed edge of a mat, or a hole in the carpet, may not be seen clearly and so cause the old person to trip. For this reason, all flooring in the dwelling should be looked at carefully, and with this particular hazard in mind. Highly-polished wooden and linoleum floorings also represent a danger and special care should be taken in the kitchen as dropped pieces of food or grease can cause a skid or fall. Electric flexes should not be allowed to trail across rooms but should be rolled up neatly and stored close to the skirting board. If there are children in the house, it is important to see that they do not leave toys and books lying on the floor. A high and consistent level of lighting is essential for elderly people, especially along passages and in w.c.'s they use during the night.

It should also be remembered that several rooms are probably used in the course of a day – as well as the sitting room, bedroom, bathroom and kitchen and sometimes the garden. Consideration has to be given to the potential danger in each one and appropriate measures taken. Handrails in the house, for instance, may be extended outdoors so that the garden can be enjoyed in safety. Organizations such as the Disabled Living Foundation and the Royal Association for Disability and Rehabilitation can advise.

Many aids and other forms of assistance are now available to make walking and bathing easier and these are discussed more fully under 'Mobility'. Waiting lists for some of these can be long, but need not mean that a much needed adaptation or aid is never going to materialize.

Even when the old person has no family to make a ramp or handrail or bath grips, there is often someone nearby who knows someone who can 'do things about the house'. There are more 'Do-it-Yourself' kits and tools on the market now than ever before. What is needed, and one of the charities or organizations concerned with old people could well supply it, is a range of instruction sheets so that ordinary people can carry out these adaptations, make these aids and undertake these repairs competently, confident that they will be one hundred per cent safe for use.

Meanwhile, organizations such as Age Concern are well worth contacting, as they often know of a volunteer with the necessary 'know-how'. Many Task Force members are also anxious to help with this kind of work. The Disabled Living Foundation have initiated various housing and design studies and feeds this newly acquired knowledge into their mine of information. They, and other Aids Centres, will also provide advice and literature on specific aids which can be demonstrated and tried out, by appointment.

If advice on safety in the home is needed, the health visitor or environmental health office should be able to help, while ROSPA (Royal Society for the Prevention of Accidents) will send an excellent check-list called 'Safety in Retirement' upon request.

Prevention of Crime and Injury by Others

Many elderly people are worried about crime and violence. Basically, there are a few simple precautions which can be taken to guard one's possessions at home and one's money when shopping.

As far as the house is concerned, one should make sure that all locks and catches are efficient. There should be a good quality mortice deadlock on all outside doors, bolts on windows, and chains on the back and front doors. If help is needed with getting these, the crime prevention officer at the local police station will give advice and the local Age Concern group will often give the necessary practical help.

When leaving home, even for a short time, it is important to close all windows (and not even leave one half-open for the cat) and never to leave a key under the doormat or on a string through the letter box. Ladders should not be left lying around and garden tools should not be left in an unlocked shed or garage. At night, it is wise to leave a light on but not just the hall light: burglars are well aware that if people are in they are not sitting in the hall.

Before going on holiday, a neighbour should be asked to 'keep an eye on things' such as noticing anyone in the garden; the lawn should be mown last thing (high grass is a give-away) and the milk and newspapers cancelled. Curtains should *not* be drawn and while the house should be locked up carefully, desks and cupboards should be left unlocked. All valuables should be deposited in the safe if there is one. It is unwise to speak in public of going away. As a precaution, in case possessions *are* stolen, it is wise to make a note of the serial numbers of the television set, transistor, camera, bicycle and record player.

Callers at the door can be a hazard: always ask for their identity cards and leave the door on its chain until satisfied that he or she is genuine. Age Concern state that suspicious statements include 'I am carrying out educational research'; 'I happened to be passing and noticed you had a loose tile on the roof'; 'I'm a consultant on back ailments and rheumatism'; 'Congratulations! my company has picked your house to be the showhouse for the area'; 'I'm selling for the blind [or disabled, or refugees or old age pensioners]'; 'I can help you cut your fuel bills'; 'I'm a student working to win a travel scholarship'; 'I'm an adviser on security . . . or fire precautions [etc.] and 'I would like to buy any antiques you have'. Even if the callers appear to be nice youngsters and say that they are 'doing a project' or offer to do odd jobs in the house, unless one knows them it is wise to telephone their school or not let them in at all.

When shopping, purses and notecases should be kept in a bag preferably with zip fastener; they should never be carried on top of the shopping bag or basket. It is also a good idea not to carry all the money in one place and to beware of pick-pockets, especially in crowds. When collecting pensions, or money from the bank or post office, try to do so at the same time as a friend and if a handbag is snatched, do not hang on to it. Where possible, keep to busy streets and avoid poorly-lit ones.

When leaving a motor-car, always lock it and remove the ignition keys; do not keep the log book, driving licence or insurance certificate in the car. (If police request them for some reason, they can be taken to the station later.) Always put any possessions into the boot of the car and lock it.

There are personal alarms available on the market and again the crime prevention officer at the local police station will be able to advise where one can be obtained locally.

Summoning Aid

Calling for aid when it is necessary has presented a problem to many old people who value and fiercely guard their independence. The fear of not being able to get to the telephone can be a great worry to them. Aid-Call, a tiny radio transmitter, is fairly expensive but is recommended. When its button is pressed it flashes a signal to a receiver in a small box of electronics by the telephone. The receiver buzzes to reassure the caller that it has received the message, then finds a GPO telephone line and 'dials' the Aid-Call Centre in London. (It can do this from anywhere in the country from which one can dial to London on STD.) At the centre (manned twenty-four hours a day all year round by specially trained people who are familiar with problems of old and disabled persons) the call is received, the code-card with its list of pre-arranged contacts (relations, friends etc.) is turned up and the Aid-Call operator telephones them. If none can be reached the operator then telephones the local police. Either way, the operator will continue to monitor the emergency until satisfied that help has reached the distressed caller.

The Aid-Call operates within a hundred yards of the control box because of its own small pull-out aerial, either in or out of doors. It is also splash (but not immersion) proof. Once purchased, it becomes the owner's property and, subject to agreement, can be re-sold. The monitoring service charge is currently forty pounds per year and, the firm, Andrew Frazer maintains it will not increase this more than the retail price index. Its advantages include the fact that as it can be worn on the wrist or as a pendant, it goes wherever the owner goes. It is the size of a watch, is sure to be heard and will not attract unwelcome visitors. The control unit is compact enough to sit unobtrusively on a table with the telephone on top.

While all these hazards and dangers may sound somewhat horrifying, one has to face the fact that we are living in a very violent, law-breaking age. It is therefore only sensible to take whatever precautions one can.

The other side of the coin is that we also live in a very technological age so we have the opportunity to acquire such electronic devices to help us. So a positive attitude even to accidents and muggings can be useful.

All through life of course our attitudes towards events, experiences and circumstances can help or hinder us and this does not change in old age.

A good example was set by a retired American journalist who wrote in a circular letter to friends: 'At 86, Rosie [his wife] and I live by the rules of the elderly. If the toothbrush is wet, you have brushed your teeth. If the bedside radio is warm in the morning, you left it on all night. If you are wearing one black shoe and one brown shoe, you have a pair like it somewhere in the closet . . . I stagger when I walk and small boys follow me, making bets on which way I will go next. This upsets me. Children should not gamble.' And so, perhaps a humorous and positive attitude can help us to cope better with certain characteristics of the ageing process. In the next chapter we will focus on a few of these.

CHAPTER 8

RESTORING FUNCTION AND IMPROVING ABILITY

Unless above himself he can
Erect himself, how poor a thing is man!

'To the Lady Margaret, Countess of Cumberland'
Samuel Daniel 1562–1619

In an article entitled 'The Old Need Cure, Not Compensation', Bob Browne suggests that we need to move away from the attitude of mind which says, 'What can we do to help?' and lays on services to compensate for observed needs of the old, to the attitude which says, 'Why does he or she need help?' and supplies the positive and remedial treatment which will operate to restore the person's function and improve or preserve his or her remaining abilities.

This chapter makes no attempt therefore to deal with specific diseases but tries to suggest some of the means and services by which an impaired function, such as hearing, can be restored and a remaining ability, such as movement, can be preserved or improved. Though we are mortal and there is no doubt that illnesses and disabilities may accumulate with age, many impaired functions and reduced abilities are signs and symptoms of the ageing process and should be dealt with as such.

Hearing

Deafness is one of the commonest examples, and one most reluctantly admitted. In their useful pamphlet, 'Why Do People Mumble So Much: No-one speaks clearly these days – or do they?' Age Concern tells us that, 'By the time we are sixty-five one out of three of us find listening and conversation difficult in everyday situations. By the time we are eighty, it is every other one of us. These are facts. But many people take a long time to realize that it is their own hearing that is causing the trouble.' They go on to say that one should not

be put off by being told that, 'becoming a bit deaf' is something which happens to most of us and one has to put up with
it.' That is not true; people in their eighties have often been
helped. But there is no need to hang on until then and the
sooner one does something about it the better. Some people
find all sounds have become muffled and quiet and that they
annoy others by turning up the radio or television and frequently asking for something to be repeated. Many others
can still hear the speaker's voice loudly enough but find it
difficult to catch all the words in a sentence. This is because
they no longer hear properly some of the consonants such as
's', 'd', 'p' and 'k'. Often they can hear a man's low voice
better than a woman or child's higher voice. They miss such
sounds as a bell ringing or the birds singing, or they have
difficulty in locating sounds in their homes.

As there are several causes of deafness at all ages, the first
step is to arrange a visit to one's GP. If wax is the cause, it
will probably be a question of putting in some drops and then
returning to have the ears syringed. If this does not improve
hearing, it may be necessary to see an ear, nose and throat
specialist in the out-patient department of the local hospital.
He may decide that a hearing aid would be helpful and for
most people different aids are issued free through the National
Health Service. Batteries and repairs are also free and a
booklet on *General Guidance for Hearing Aid Users* is provided.
A good number of people have been persuaded to spend a lot
of money buying an aid privately and then find it is no better
than the NHS one. If you do want to buy an aid (and it is
true that there is a long waiting list for the NHS behind-
the-ear fitted aids), seek advice from the hospital's hearing
aid centre. Beware of answering advertisements, buying from
an exhibition or from a travelling salesman who comes to the
door. However satisfactory an aid may seem, insist on a trial
period of at least one week before buying it. Never sign an
agreement without reading the small print and remember
that the most expensive aid is not necessarily the best nor the
most suitable.

It is also important to remember that a hearing aid is,
literally, an aid to hearing and will make all sounds louder.
No hearing aid restores natural hearing: it will amplify all
sounds just as a magnifying glass amplifies all print. An aid
is most effective when the speaker is not more than seven feet

away and there is little background noise, such as traffic or the chatter of crowds. It is helpful to stand or sit with the light behind, so that the speaker's face can be seen clearly for most of us 'hear' better if we see the speaker. (This is one reason why telephone conversations can be difficult.) Tiled walls, shiny and polished surfaces create echoes and make hearing more difficult; soft furnishings on the other hand absorb these, which means that an aid needs to be adjusted according to the situation. This may take some time to judge and manipulate and is another reason why it is better to begin to use one at an early stage.

The local social services department will be able to give help and advice. Some have a specialist social worker for the deaf who may also be able to provide an interpreting service, either sign language or lip-reading, for important occasions when it is vital to know what is being said. One or two voluntary organizations also provide a similar interpreting service.

Those who live with, or have contact with, someone who has difficulty in hearing can help considerably by speaking distinctly and putting their faces in a good light so that the mouth and lips can be seen clearly. (Hands, cigarettes and pipes can obstruct the view.) Shouting distorts both the voice and the mouth, so often adds to the difficulty – and causes embarrassment. If the hearing of one ear is better than the other, remember which it is and speak into that.

Sight

Changes in sight occur with ageing and most of us have to take to wearing spectacles in our fifties or even in our forties. If vision begins to fail, however, the GP should be consulted in order to exclude the possibility of disease. There are some eye diseases which occur in old age but which do not affect vision in the early stages. For this reason it is wise after the age of fifty, to have one's eyes examined by a qualified ophthalmic optician at least every two years, whether one wears spectacles or not. Dispensing opticians only dispense the lenses prescribed and make up the spectacles; they are not qualified to examine and prescribe. One examination a year is free under the NHS. If the ophthalmic optician or surgeon finds more are necessary, they can also be carried out free of charge. Old people who receive supplementary pensions and some others with small incomes are entitled to free spectacles or spectacles at a reduced rate, depending upon the frames chosen. Opticians will have the appropriate form of application and this should be completed and sent to the local social security office.

Spectacles alone may not be sufficient for someone who is partially sighted. He or she may need a vision aid such as a hand magnifier, a stand magnifier or a special telescope. In some instances, these can be obtained through the NHS. They may be expensive to buy and an expert opinion should be sought before doing so.

Registration as a partially sighted or blind person is a voluntary decision and an ophthalmologist can advise and assess accordingly. If appropriate, a certificate is then sent to the social services department to place the name and address of the person on the relevant register The latter should result in a visit from a social worker who will be able to discuss individual problems arising from the loss of sight and ways and means of overcoming them.

In some parts of the country, there are teachers or technical staff who will provide practical help such as teaching the blind person to dress, how to ensure that they put on the clothes they want to, or how to shave or make-up. They may also help with teaching the blind person to use talking books and tape recorders. The British Talking Book Service offers a range of books recorded on cassettes. These are sent free of charge from the library who will also supply the special play-back machine. The annual subscription for this service is paid by the library or by the local authority social services department. The latter may also pay for telephones for blind people but financial resources do not cover this in all parts of the country. The Telephones for the Blind Fund may be able to help in some instances.

Help may also be needed with mobility and the social services department will be able to help by supplying a white stick, giving relevant traning or suggesting a guide dog. Training in its use can be provided either locally or at a residential social-rehabilitation centre.

Blind people are also able to obtain a higher level of supplementary benefit. In some instances attendance allowance may be paid, while the carer may be able to apply for an

invalid care allowance. Further information can be obtained
from the local social security office and much useful advice
on the whole subject is contained in the leaflet 'Your Sight
and the National Health Service', also available from the
department's local office. Other sources of help, according to
interest, need, place of residence and occupation are listed in
the Appendix. Relatives and friends of partially-sighted or
blind people sometimes need to be reminded that loss of sight
does not mean a loss of hearing or a loss of presence. So many
blind people are either shouted at or referred to in the third
person, not being allowed to speak for themselves. It is helpful
to give blind or partially-sighted people some idea of where
one is sitting, standing, moving to and also what one is doing.

Speech

Speech problems sometimes occur after a stroke and may
require expertise from a speech therapist. Family and friends
can also help. Powers of recovery are often underestimated:
constant practice can bring surprising rewards. Reading
aloud, singing, listening to the wireless or television, and
playing records or word games will all help and the speech
therapist and health visitor are there to advise and support.

The right approach and practice in the home can help
enormously but there are a few points which are worth remembering. It is helpful to speak slowly and distinctly and
to allow the affected person also to speak slowly. Do not
interrupt or try to finish a sentence because the whole train
of his or her thought as well as speech will be interrupted.

Childish speech does not mean childish thinking: the ability
to communicate thought may be affected but the intelligence
need not be. The inability to communicate what one wants
to say can cause anger, frustration, depression and if allowed
to do so, isolation. Sometimes when there is difficulty in
communicating with others, there is also difficulty in communicating with oneself. Others, who are able to understand
what is being said, will become infuriated when unable to
respond in words or sentences. Under such circumstances,
errors may be made, or one word may be repeated time and
time again, or the response to all questions may be the same,
using the wrong word. Often the harder a person tries the
more upset he or she is when it comes out wrong. Listeners

must be sensitive and patient and that is not easy day after day. Support and encouragement from all members of the family, from friends and from members of the social and health services will be needed.

Other sources of help include the Association for Dysphasic Adults, the Amandus Club (associated with the Atkinson Morley Hospital and concerned with the rehabilitation of 'stroke' patients)the Chest, Heart and Stroke Association, the Cicely Northcote Trust (which maintains a register of speech clubs), the College of Speech Therapists (which publishes pamphlets for patients and families), while some of the organizations who supply talking books for blind and partially-sighted people will also lend them to others. Records of plays with the scripts spoken by professional actors are especially helpful in this context.

Teeth are important for speaking as well as for eating and appearance. Every national of this country is allowed two free dental examinations each year. Unfortunately, in some areas it is difficult to obtain the services of a dentist under the NHS; because of the lower rate of pay the government makes to them, some accept only private patients. If difficulty is experienced, it is sometimes worth writing to the dental officer at the local health authority or to the local branch of Age Concern or enquiring at the local Citizens Advice Bureau; any of these may know of a local dentist who accepts NHS patients.

People who receive supplementary pensions are entitled to free dental treatment. Others, whose income is a little above this level, may also be eligible for financial help. The dentist himself will have the appropriate form which should be completed and returned to the local social security office. Two useful information leaflets which are available from post offices are 'NHS Dental Treatment', and 'Free! if you are on a low income: dental treatment, glasses, milk and vitamins, prescriptions.'

Dentures
Some old people do not have dentures replaced when they need to and as gums shrink with age, this results in ill-fitting teeth. Both speech and eating become increasingly difficult, the former resulting in poor communication and the latter in

malnutrition. Ill-fitting dentures can also cause sores and ulcers of the mouth and tongue. New or replaced dentures take getting used to but confidence can be built up by reading aloud in front of a looking glass. A greater sense of security can also be gained by using a denture fixative: the dentist will advise. Cleaning requires more than steeping the dentures in a fluid overnight: a special brush and dentifrice are essential if dentures are to be clean and comfortable and one's breath to remain sweet and fresh. If there are other needs or difficulties associated with treatment of teeth or dentures, the local Citizens Advice Bureau or branch of Age Concern will advise where to go for help.

Memory

A failing memory is the symptom of ageing which most of us notice first. It is important to differentiate between this and the impairment of logical thinking. The latter can result in mistakes being made in the conversation, such as talking about the wrong day of the week. Whenever such an error is made, it should be referred to and gently corrected. Throughout life, family, friends and colleagues do this and old age should not merit an exception. Sometimes one is tempted to agree because it is quicker and possibly because it seems to be more polite. But, in the long term this can have serious consequences: a person who is never corrected will stray further from reality. Repetition can be tiring and infuriating, especially when correction has little effect. At that point it is better to change the subject. Even if a state of confusion seems to exist (and there is a good deal of confusion about the use of that word), and childish things are spoken, an old person should never be spoken to as though he were in a second childhood. Even babyish terms of affection can be insulting. Confusional states are characterized by a disturbance of memory, the inability to recognize time and place and the loss of practical skills such as coherent speech, dressing and continence. More florid symptoms may develop such as restlessness (day or night) – which sometimes results in wanderings away from home, aggressiveness and hallucinations. Many old people are treated successfully at home, depending upon the diagnosis. A geriatric physician or a psychogeriatrician should be consulted as soon as possible.

While errors in speech can be corrected, attention drawn to a lack of memory may lead to anxiety and depression. Help can be given by 'jogging' the failing memory. For instance, instead of saying, 'Here's your weekend shopping', one can say, 'Here's your meat for Sunday lunch', or instead of 'I've just seen Miss Pettigrew', one can elaborate, 'I've just seen my old headmistress, Miss Pettigrew'. Memory-joggings of this kind are vitally important, otherwise in time the gas fire may be turned on and not lighted, bills may remain unpaid and appointments forgotten. Written instructions are more effective than verbal ones and the whole family can make efforts to improve the 'sensory environment'. Calendars with very large figures and writing can be helpful with special dates ringed in red. Chiming clocks are constant reminders of time and alarm clocks can be set at meal times. If areas or doors are painted in different colours it will help people to identify their surroundings and increase the 'patterning of sensory input'. Imagination is needed and the younger members of the family should be brought in to contribute their own ideas. As they watch the old person respond to them, they will not only become interested but also obtain some degree of delight.

One defect which can be exhausting is the repeated questioning or action. While it can be a memory defect, it sometimes is a means of gaining attention. It should be stressed, however, that this is equally unconscious behaviour; the old person does not realize what he or she is doing nor why he or she is doing it. Expert advice is necessary when this happens and the local doctor may ask the psychiatric community nurse to advise or consult a psychiatrist.

Disorientation can be a sign of depression as well as one of brain failure. To be orientated we must be able to hear, see and communicate, so it is important to ensure that old people are able to function to their fullest capability.

It is useful to remember too, that swings of mood increase with age, and in some old people as the brain fails, the emotional response to a remark or event may be out of all proportion or even inappropriate. A sharp word can bring tears or anger, or result in shouting and great distress. To prevent such emotional outbursts it is important for all those in contact with such an old person to remain, proverbially, 'cool, calm and collected', which is easy to say but not so easy to do. If the situation becomes difficult, advice should be sought from the social worker, health visitor or other professional who knows the old person. While occasional arguments and loss of temper are normal, emotional upsets should not become frequent nor be allowed to continue, for the Welfare State exists to provide help.

Mobility

A decrease in personal mobility is inevitable as age increases, for while old age in itself is not a cause, illnesses which occur during it often are. If mobility lessens considerably over a short period such as a month or so, if joints and muscles are painful or if movement is impaired so that self-help is not possible, the GP should be consulted in order that underlying disease can be diagnosed and treated. Cure may not always be possible for conditions such as Parkinson's disease, rheumatoid arthritis, brain, lung or heart disease, but impaired movement can often be improved with help from physiotherapists, occupational therapists, pharmacotherapy, and the use of various special aids, gadgets and appliances. In addition to advice from the primary health team (domiciliary nurses, health visitors and social workers as well as doctors and therapists) many associations and organizations exist to help specific groups of people. These are listed in the Appendix.

As well as receiving help from a 'speciality' organization one can also give help in discussion with others, either those who have the illness or condition themselves, or with their families and friends. Such mutual-help interest groups are increasing in number and the local Age Concern group should have knowledge of those in their area.

For people who have arthritis, help may be made available through the local GP, from a rheumatologist or a specialist in physical medicine. Sometimes surgery, such as hip replacement, may be advised. If the arthritis is causing difficulty with daily-living activities such as washing or cooking, a domiciliary occupational therapist, a social services department or Aids Centre should be able to advise on the various forms of practical and financial help available.

Various aids and adaptations are possible and descriptions of these can be obtained either from the Information Service at the Disabled Living Foundation or other Aids Centres. Local professionals will be able to advise on which are the most suitable, and 'Best Buys for the Handicapped' by Newton Aids, gives descriptions of comparative quality, strength and reliability. *Which* magazine can also be consulted. Before buying any aid, however, it is well worth discovering which can be obtained through the health service or hired from a voluntary organization. As well as bath boards and w.c. seats, there are hoists, rails, walking frames and simple devices to facilitate turning taps, cutting bread and meat, peeling potatoes and fruit, opening tins and packages, dressing and drying oneself, putting on socks or stockings, gardening and knitting, picking up dropped articles and even sponge-sticks for washing feet and long horns for putting on shoes. There are also gadgets to help with eating and drinking. Cutlery with thick handles is easier to grasp or, alternatively, the local branch of the Red Cross will supply tube-sponge for adapting ordinary knives, spoons and forks. There are also non-slip mats for putting underneath plates and dishes (Dycem plastic pads), specially designed 'safe' kettles, saucepans, teapots and so on. The Disabled Living Foundation will send information sheets by post, while the Arthritis Care (in association with the Lady Hoare Trust) publishes its own newspaper containing invaluable information, advice and news of recent developments. Shower units and bidets can be very useful in certain cases. Alternatively, in some districts, there are day centres or hospitals where disabled old people can go to be bathed.

The British Gas Home Service Department will advise on the choice and installation of gas appliances for disabled people and also supply a range of special aids and adaptors. The Electricity Council has produced a leaflet with the co-operation of the Disabled Living Foundation on 'Making Life Easier for Disabled People' which gives advice on heaters, cookers, hot water and laundry, including details of some of the special controls which can be fitted to appliances such as cookers. Copies of the leaflet are free from local electricity board showrooms or direct from the Electricity Council.

The Women's Royal Voluntary Service (WRVS) and the Disabled Living Foundation publish a guide on adapting clothes for disabled people and the latter have a clothing adviser who will give help with individual difficulties. Special clothing is also on the market and the Shirley Institute publishes a catalogue listing designs and their suppliers.

Visiting friends and relations when disabled can present problems. Adjustment to a different height of chair or w.c. may be difficult at first, as will the depth of unfamiliar steps or stairs. Most of us have experienced that unpleasant feeling when a seat or step has been higher or lower than we were expecting. One geriatrician has commented that an elderly person may be compared with a rock climber for whom a missed footing means a fall. Such adjustments will take him or her a little time, for, as explained earlier, new information takes longer to retain at this stage of life. Patience is likely to be needed all round, and for some months.

One deterrent to mobility may be loss of spring in the feet caused by fallen arches. If combined with arthritic problems of the knees or hip, walking may become somewhat of a shuffle which will make uneven floors, polished linoleum, poly-vinyl tiles, frayed or torn carpets, and loose rugs or mats even more hazardous. People who find mobility difficult must be able to reach, manipulate and use those features of their environment which are important to them.

All furniture which provides sitting surfaces, including a commode, must be to hand and of the correct or convenient height. A wide variety of furniture for the disabled or immobile person is available now, and again the Disabled Living Foundation will provide information sheets and advice upon request.

Immobility can lead to joint stiffness and muscle weakness. This results in less movement and so the vicious circle is set up.

Loss of Bladder Control

The word incontinence is used when control of the bladder or bowel, or of both, is weakened or lost. Although incontinence can affect all ages, older people sometimes feel they have to suffer it, and that nothing can be done. They may feel a need to pass water more frequently and sometimes with great urgency, and problems can arise when some loss of mobility or increased physical frailty also have to be taken into account. It may take too long to reach the lavatory, for instance, (especially if it is up or down a flight of stairs) and accidents may result. Severe constipation can be a cause of incontinence of urine.

Here are some helpful suggestions:

 i) A commode can be kept conveniently near, either beside the bed or in the living room. There are some types designed to look like ordinary fireside chairs. A portable toilet (chemical closet) is another solution.

 ii) For those confined to bed or chair, a bedpan or urinal may prove more suitable. There are a variety of designs, some of which can be managed quite easily without help.

 iii) Make sure that the bladder is emptied as completely as possible. Bending forward helps this process, so in this respect using a lavatory or commode has advantages, provided there is no risk of overbalancing. For those with stiff hips a raised lavatory seat makes getting on and off easier; a grab rail fastened to the wall is also a great help.

 iv) The bladder tends to respond to a routine, so it should be emptied at regular intervals, whether or not an urge is felt. A two-hour pattern suits most people – to avoid forgetting, an alarm clock or kitchen 'pinger' can be used.

 v) It is very important to drink the normal amount; contrary to what one might expect, cutting down on fluids may make matters worse. It is advisable to drink plenty in the earlier part of the day, but to have the last drink two or three hours before bedtime.

 vi) It is also very important to avoid constipation; although individual bowel habits can vary greatly – between once or twice a day and two or three times a week – the main thing is regularity. It is important to drink plenty, and try to include fresh fruit and vegetables in the diet, and bran in bread or breakfast cereals.

 vii) Clothing and nightwear can be chosen or adapted for easier management, and some suggestions on this are obtainable from the Incontinence Advisory Service of the Disabled Living Foundation.

Faecal Incontinence

Loss of control over the action of the bowel can be very distressing, but a bowel motion occurs less frequently than the need to pass water. Attention to possible causes may help to prevent it happening, or at least to make control more possible.

i) One of the most common types of faecal incontinence, known as 'overflow diarrhoea', is caused, perhaps surprisingly, by severe constipation. It is important therefore, especially for those who are inactive, to avoid becoming constipated; plenty of fluid and a good mixed diet which includes protein, fruit and fresh vegetables, and perhaps a bran breakfast cereal is recommended. Sometimes a glass of hot water in the morning or evening will help to stimulate the movement of the bowel. If severe constipation exists, the doctor or nurse may consider it necessary to clear out the bowel by means of suppositories or enema. When this has been done, and a regular routine which suits the individual has been established, the important thing is to maintain some degree of regularity.

Incontinence of urine may in some cases also be the result of severe constipation, and the same treatment will be required.

ii) Persistent diarrhoea can arise for a number of different reasons, and always call for medical advice.

iii) If, as sometimes happens, control of the bowel cannot be restored, there is still much that can be done to increase comfort and peace of mind. Much use can be made of disposable protective materials, both for the person and for the bed, and these are normally supplied and delivered free of charge through the Health Services. The home Nurse or Health Visitor will help and advise in regard to these arrangements. In some areas collection of used pads is also undertaken.

Disposable garments recommended for faecal incontinence
Cumfies: – disposable napkin type, with waterproof cover and self-fastening patches.
Molnycke Maxi-Snibb and Pad: – disposable highly absorbent pad & soft plastic bikini which ties at each hip.

Aids

Commodes and Chemical Closets

If the lavatory is not easily accessible a commode or chemical closet can be a substitute. A chemical closet has the advantage of needing less frequent emptying; on the other hand some commodes are made to look like well designed chairs, and can be kept in the bedroom or living room as part of the ordinary furniture.

Commodes

The following points should be considered when choosing a commode:

i) The height should be the same as that of the bed or wheelchair for ease of movement from one to the other. The usual height is 18″, but some types are adjustable.

ii) It is important that it should be the right height for the user to sit comfortably, with both feet firmly on the floor.

iii) It should have a firm base with legs wider than the arms. A type with arms and backrest is usually best, but where the user transfers sideways, a type with a removable or swinging arm can be obtained.

iv) Where a commode needs to be moved, some types have castors, or wheels which can be braked when in use.

v) A sani-chair may be convenient; this is a lavatory seat seat in a chair on wheels, so that the user can be wheeled, or can propel himself, over a lavatory or commode. Before acquiring one of these the height of the lavatory must be measured to ensure that the sani-chair will go over it.

vi) For those who are alone and unable to move the Easi-nurse cushion can be a solution. It is a specially designed cushion with an opening beneath which a bedpan or receptacle is placed.

Chemical Closets

There are many different types and sizes. Those with a smaller capacity are lighter for emptying, but may tend to be less stable, and sometimes too low for a heavy or disabled user.

Aids in the Lavatory

For those who have difficulty in bending, a raised lavatory seat makes sitting and getting up easier. There are various types which raise the height of the seat by 4″ to 6″. They can easily be lifted off for ordinary use.

Support Rails

Suitably placed rails can provide support and assistance to the elderly or disabled while getting up and down, and when managing clothing. *Grab rails* can be affixed to the wall, and there are various types of *toilet support rails and bars*, some fixed to the wall and some to the floor. One example is a drop-down bar fastened to the wall with a drop-down self-locking right-angled leg; it can be folded back against the wall to give access to wheelchair users. There are also chrome rails which provide all-round support to the frail or unsteady; the *Mecan-aid Toilet aid*, which can be locked in place through the mounting holes of the lavatory seat, has arms which close across the front of the user, hinged to swing out of the way for getting on and off.

Special aids for bathing and washing:

Where the incontinent person is also disabled, a hoist can assist with lifting. There are special seats which fit inside or over the bath, and others which can be used with a simple shower hose.

Supply of aids:

In many cases aids of the kind described here can be supplied through the local authority, the social services department or by the local health district. The family doctor, district nurse or health visitor, or the local social services department should be able to advise on equipment helpful in your particular situation.

The Disabled Living Foundation and Information Service List No. 7A 'Personal Toilet' gives details of aids and equipment available, with details of manufacturers, suppliers, guide to current prices etc. Many items are on display at the Foundation's Aids Centre, to which visits can be made by appointment.

Clothing

For those who are incontinent, the choice of clothing not only affects appearance and therefore morale, but can contribute greatly to making the condition more manageable.

It is wise to avoid heavy or non-washable fabrics: modern synthetics which are easily washed and dried and require little or no pressing are a boon to the incontinent of both sexes.

Styles can be chosen or adapted for ease of handling, and difficulty with fastenings can be lessened by the use of Velcro, zips, or large buttons.

Some suggestions:

For women

For those who need to pass water quickly, a full skirt is easier and quicker to pull up than a close fitting one, and knicker elastic should be fairly loose. Easy fitting slacks with an elasticated waistband are also more quickly pulled down than slacks with fasteners.

Women who wear protective padding may find a loose-fitting three quarter length top or jacket over slacks or skirt is helpful in concealing any bulges. Skirts and nightdresses which open at the back are useful for those people who are confined to a wheelchar or to a bed.

For men

Trousers with a long fly facilitate using a bottle. One example is the Edgware trouser. This also has a long back seam which is more comfortable for a man who is confined to sitting for long periods in a wheelchair. These trousers are made in various colours in drip-dry material and can be ordered in any size from D. B. Thomas and Son Ltd. For the man who wears a urinary collecting device and leg-bag, a zip fastener in the trouser leg seam allows for each emptying and changing of the bag.

For those of either sex who are physically handicapped and experience particular difficulties in managing clothing, especially for toilet purposes, there are specially designed garments of adaptations which can be made. Ideas as well as information can be found in the Disabled Living Foundation's book *Clothes Sense for Handicapped Adults of all Ages* by P. Macartney, available from the Disabled Living Foundation. List

13 on 'Clothing' from the same source also gives useful advice, while the Clothing Adviser of the Disabled Living Foundation will provide general information upon personal request.

Other relevant information lists published by the Disabled Living Foundation's Information Service include: Notes on Incontinence; List 12: Incontinence Aids and Protective Pads; and List 1: Beds. The latter includes information on mattresses, protective plastics of various kinds, drawsheets, one-way sheeting, disposable and other bedding and anti-pressure equipment. Fuller information may also be obtained from an illustrated handbook 'Incontinence: A guide to the Understanding and Management of a Very Common Complaint' by Dorothy Mandelstam, which is available from the Disabled Living Foundation. Confidential enquiries about individual incontinence problems not dealt with in 'Notes on Incontinence' may be made by letter to the Incontinence Adviser at the Foundation. The prices of all Disabled Living Foundation lists and publications ae available on request.

Colostomies and Ileostomies
For people who have recently had, or are about to have, a colostomy or ileostomy operation, the stoma therapist should be consulted. Organizations which also give useful advice and information are the Colostomy Welfare Group; the Ileostomy Association of Great Britain and Northern Ireland and the Urinary Conduit Association. For day-to-day help, the local GP and health visitor should be contacted.

Aids Centres
The range of aids available to help disabled people overcome residual disability is now extensive and this, together with the complexity of some of the equipment, means even greater skill is needed to select the right aid or aids for any problem. The purpose of aids centres is not to sell aids, but to provide a resource facility where aids can be seen and tried out. There are now twelve such centres throughout the country and also three travelling ones, which move around from site to site, visiting areas which have no permanent centre. Although each centre is autonomous all have the same basic aims.

The first aim is to provide information on aids, equipment

and related subjects to all those professionally concerned with
the rehabilitation or care of disabled people. The centres can
be used either for postgraduate teaching or as resource centres
where staff can keep up to date with new equipment.

The second aim is to provide a teaching facility for students.
It is difficult to appreciate how a piece of equipment works
without actually being able to see it and to discuss its application. Hoists, for instance, are necessary both in hospitals
and in the home for lifting and transferring severely disabled
people. There are many different types of hoist and many
different designs of sling and the techniques for using them
depend on the person and the situation. Unless students have
an opportunity to see the range, try them out and become
familiar with their use, they will be unable to cope adequately
in circumstances where a hoist is necessary. The same applies
to the range of wheelchairs, environmental controls, bathroom
equipment and all the other equipment disabled people need
to use.

The third aim is to provide a showroom for disabled people
themselves. Many disabled people and their families know
exactly what they want; others may not, but may still wish
to find out the information for themselves, rather than rely
on the statutory sources. An aids centre provides them with
the opportunity to see equipment, to try it out and to discuss,
in a non-commercial and non-medical setting, the features
that are relevant to their particular problem.

Although these centres were set up primarily to provide
information on equipment, it became evident that most visitors needed more than this. It is seldom that an aid can be
used in isolation. For instance, a person enquiring about a
wheelchair will need to know not only about the different
types of wheelchair available, but also where to obtain one,
how to use it, how to lift it into the boot of a car, how to
transfer from the chair to the bed, how to maintain the wheelchair and what adaptations to the house are likely to be
necessary. In addition, anyone who uses a wheelchair all day
and every day may well be entitled to various allowances, or
perhaps to a rate rebate. The person may want to discuss the
problems which will arise when travelling, or may want to
know about training or employment possibilities. To help
with such advice, most aids centres are backed up by both

the Information Service at the Disabled Living Foundation and by their own local information services.

Aids centres vary considerably in size and content but all provide a basic resource centre on disabled living. Visits are free for elderly and disabled people but it is always necessary to make an appointment (except when visiting the travelling aids centres). A list of centres may be obtained from the Joint Aids Centres Committee, c/o the Disabled Living Foundation.

As can be seen, many organizations, associations and trusts exist solely to help those people who have a specific disability or diminishing function. One can only make sure that these people receive the relevant information concerning the services and benefits which are available, for each person must be allowed to live as he or she wishes, even if it involves risk to health or life. While no human being has complete freedom of action, each has the right to refuse help and advice at any age. The right to take risks in old age is a very important issue and the following chapter is an attempt to synthesize some of the current thinking on the subject.

PART III

ACCEPTING DEPENDENCE

The value of Life lies not in the length of days, but in the use you make of them: he has lived for a long time who has little lived. Whether you have lived enough depends not on the number of your years, but on your will.

Montaigne 1533–1592

CHAPTER 9

RUNNING RISKS AND HAVING RIGHTS

Margaret: 'She must be lost'
Nicholas: 'Who isn't? The best
Thing we can do is to make wherever we're lost in
Look as much like home as we can.'

A Sleep of Prisoners
Christopher Fry 1951

Liberty is an elusive concept. No human being has complete freedom of action. Ordinary people are constrained by work, income, housing and a host of other factors which limit the range of courses open to them. For those who are frail or disabled and living on a pension, what they might like to do and what is physically or financially possible, diverge still further. It would be unrealistic not to realize that this is inevitable. Alison Norman, Deputy Director of the Centre for Policy on Ageing, writes, 'However, there are ways in which society further restricts this narrowing range of choice by imposing on elderly people forms of care and treatment which are the fruit of social perception, social anxiety, convenience or custom, rather than inescapable necessity.' She goes on to say, 'Old people are taken from their homes when domiciliary supported physical treatment might enable them to stay there; they are subjected in long stay hospitals and homes to régimes which deprive them of many basic human dignities; and they are often not properly consulted about the care or treatment to which they are subjected.'

Disabled old people are competing with other members of society for finite resources, both statutory and voluntary, both emotional and physical. Carers also have rights and the needs and claims of others (children, mentally and physically handicapped people) are acknowledged. Yet surely old people should be offered alternatives better than those which we so often present to them. At the present time, when standards of housing and levels of domiciliary support and treatment are not sufficient to make possible a reasonable level of

warmth, cleanliness and nutrition, 'disabled old people have
as little choice in whether or not to give up their homes as if
they had been ordered away from them under Section 47 of
the National Assistance Act'.

A more skilled, varied and sensitive use of limited resources
is called for, not a massive increase of them. Above all, an
underlying shift in attitudes towards old people is needed: a
shift away from the patronizing and paternalistic overprotec-
tion from risk, and a shift towards the acknowledgement of
their right to as much self-determination as is possible for
each individual to have, within the limits of resources
available.

Society is not consistent in the risks it allows and those
against which it attempts to defend itself. Some people are
allowed to take risks, others are prevented from doing so. For
example, mountain-climbing and pot-holing are 'allowed' to
continue in spite of grumbles about the cost of rescue operations, a number of hospital treatments and an occasional fatal
accident. Yet paraplegic people are often prevented from using public buildings because they might not be able to escape
if there was a fire and the lifts were immobilized. Their own
wish to accept the risk is ignored.

Society also treats people in institutions differently from the
way it treats individuals. People in their own houses are not
compelled to have fire extinguishers. Yet crippling demands
are made for fire precautions in homes for old people, demands which force fees to be raised to a level which residents
find hard (sometimes impossible) to meet, impose barriers on
their mobility and sometimes force homes to close or other
services to be drastically reduced. The residents are never
asked what level of risk they themselves consider acceptable,
and how they rate the danger of burning to death as compared
with the danger of homelessness because they can no longer
afford the fees, or the danger of immobilization because they
cannot get through the fire door with their walking frames.

When one comes to questions of individual risk and protection the problems become even more complex. As Paul
Brearley has pointed out:

> The practitioner's life is not made any easier by the general
> nature of much of the legislation. The National Assistance
> Act, for instance, speaks of 'care and attention'; the Health

Services and Public Health Act, of promoting the welfare of the elderly, while the most recent memorandum on health services in old people's homes of 'support', 'care' and 'attention'. The extent and nature of social workers' duty to *protect* old people is unclear and their vulnerability to criticism is consequently heightened.

The practitioner thus has to take into account potential damage to his own personal and professional reputation as well as possible danger to others and danger to the person who is seen to be 'at risk'. We need, Alison Norman declares, 'much better analytical tools for assessing the hazards, dangers and *strengths* of a particular situation so that the risks involved in action or inaction can be properly weighed up'. Brearley has done some innovative work in this field and his analytical framework for the assessment of risk could become a basic tool in the training of social workers. Again, the old persons' own wish to accept risk should not be ignored just to salve our own consciences.

The risks of choosing what we may consider the 'safest' solution for old people are illustrated in an article published recently in the British Medical Journal. In 'Slow euthanasia or "she'll be better off in hospital" ', Alex Baker writes:

An old lady lives alone with a neglected garden and a dilapidated house. She has gradually lost her contacts with the outside world, and the circle of friends and neighbours who had helped her with shopping and visits has diminished as she has become increasingly dirty and neglected. She has discouraged home-help and meals-on-wheels services and is now living in squalor and is perhaps incontinent.

Her memory is failing and her general health is becoming frail. She may already be known to the police because of wandering from the house, and neighbours and others have begun to put pressure on the medical and social services to have her removed. An incident such as a fall in the house, a fire, another episode of wandering, or fear of hypothermia has brought the firm request that she should be admitted to hospital.

Admission is arranged sometimes by simple persuasion of a muddled old lady and sometimes by use of Section 25 of the Mental Health Act, or some other legal framework.

Most of those concerned feel a sense of relief and say to themselves 'she'll be better off in hospital'. There, it is usually argued, she will be safer, have a longer life and better medical and nursing care. The facts, however, are not so comforting.

The author goes on to say that in the psychiatric hospital where he works, it has been found that 25 per cent of old people of this kind die within three weeks of admission, although most are physically healthy when admitted. The cause of death is usually a terminal broncho-pneumonia. The pattern of events leading up to death is often similar. Again, the author describes it from his own experience:

The old person is admitted, bathed, re-dressed and within twenty-four hours may be hardly recognizable as the same person as the dirty, tattered old woman, crouched at home by her fire. On the other hand, the old woman who crouched by the fire, often had a good deal to say for herself, showed both individuality and determination, and could be self-assertive.

In hospital, however, the same old woman may appear bewildered, restless, look around in perplexity and seem unable to express any need other than, perhaps, the desire to go home. The initial restlessness, often wandering around the ward, looking in vain for familiar places or people, will give way to apathy and dejection. This may happen spontaneously, but it may also be induced by medication. In the phase of apathy, the appetite is often diminished, incontinence develops and physical frailty (sometimes with falls), becomes more obvious. At some point, either after a fall, or because a change in the old lady's appearance causes concern, she is put to bed. Within a day or two, she develops chest symptoms and dies a day or two later.

Some, of course, survive the shock of hospital admission, but the author questions whether these people are 'better off' than they would be in their own home:

The patients are totally dependent upon the nurses for their survival. Nurses take obvious pride and pleasure in attending to their patients' basic needs, often addressing them by special names or endearments. The similarity between care required by a newborn baby is, of course, striking. Some patients seem to survive in a totally demented and dependent state for several years thanks to the most excellent and devoted nursing care. Death, however, cannot be evaded for ever, and the final months of many of these patients' lives can be very distressing.

Life is extended, but for what purpose? Again, the author of the article in the British Medical Journal describes in detail the long drawn-out and painful dying of one such old lady. He concludes:

> There can be no doubt that the life of some of these elderly patients is considerably extended by nursing and medical care. There must be considerable doubt whether this extension is in any sense beneficial to the patient. Skilled nursing care can maintain life in a frail, elderly patient, whose general condition is such that a comparable state in an animal might well lead to prosecution of the owner. . . Senile dementing processes sometimes lead to a relatively quick and peaceful death. Many, however, particularly under modern conditions of treatment, can be very cruel illnesses. The problems of dying, particularly in patients with pain from tumours, have been discussed fairly widely recently, and there is now a much better understanding of the process and of the medical and nursing approach that is needed. There is a similar need to discuss the problems of dying when there is no acute process and a prolonged terminal phase is likely. Cruelty to the elderly can take many forms.

In her excellent discussion document, 'Rights and Risks', Alison Norman asks some of the questions illustrated in this article. How far should old people be allowed to live in squalor if they refuse help? What level of danger or inconvenience to neighbours outweighs an individual's right to remain in his own home? What use should be made of compulsion under the Mental Health Act or the National Assistance Act? How does one balance the risks of institutionalization against the risks of remaining independent? How can institutional care preserve the identity of those being cared for? How can the care of dying people be improved? How can the legal and social rights of mentally disabled old people be protected?

Leaving aside those old people who, like members of any age group, are admitted to hospital for treatment or investigations which cannot be carried out at home, it would seem that the majority are admitted to institutions because their relatives want it and not because they do. It is a fact that amongst those who are admitted to hospital, it is those who live alone who find it easiest to obtain discharge. Yet these are often the people at greatest risk. There are reasons of course, and the main one is that the 'social space' which has been occupied by the old person before admission, often closes, unless it is his or her own home. The family may suddenly feel very relieved and realize, perhaps for the first time, that he or she has become a burden to them. They agree among themselves that they cannot have the person back. A landlord may take the opportunity to get in a younger tenant who will not be 'such a bother and responsibility', or the warden of a sheltered housing home may declare that she, 'can't cope with all the nursing he needs'.

It goes without saying that, ideally, elderly people in care should enjoy, 'the liberty granted to any other adult citizen to order his activities, finances and personal affairs, subject only to restrictions which are necessary in order to provide the level of care he needs, or to protect the quality of life of other residents and of the care givers'. At least one local authority has attempted to draw up a written contract which is agreed when residents enter its home. The fact that it is necessary is somewhat worrying but at least the need has been recognized and acknowledged by one Council.

The Residential Care Association stated in its comments on the DHSS discussion document 'A Happier Old Age':

An enormous amount of work still needs to be done in improving the amount of personal freedom open to residents in residential accommodation. Some of the 'better' homes are attempting to maintain human dignity and preserve freedom wherever possible, but far too often the attitude remains that when people come into care they become subject to the system and to the needs of the staff, which involves a massive loss of personal dignity and individual freedom. Examples are lack of choice of menu, the inability to come and go outside the home, staff always present during bathing time, set meal times etc. We believe that residents should be able to keep their own pension books, choose the type of food they eat, to come and go in the residential establishment as they please, get up and go to bed at times which suit themselves, have meal times over a flexible period, choose their own clothes, have access to meal and snack facilities, please themselves if and when they have a bath (subject to the need to bath relatively frequently), have access to private facilities where they can receive relatives and friends, and also be actively encouraged to take a hand in the running of the home.

We appreciate that for some residents a free life involves some amount of risk, but risk is part of normal life and it must be accepted by both social services departments, members and residential staff that independent living should be encouraged even though there are elements of risk.

Improvement is slow, for a number of reasons. Some buildings are unsuitable, many old people are very old, costs are rising all the time, there is a shortage of staff for this kind of work, and so on. But as in any setting, the quality of care depends upon the quality of staff, and the guidance, pride and encouragement of them depend upon their employers, whether local authority, a voluntary committee or a private owner. If they, as domestic staff, cooks and gardeners, are accorded low status and offered low pay in this setting, it will be reflected in their own self-estimation, perception and confidence. Yet, as Alison Norman has said, 'The best examples of residential care show how much can be done to make the last years of people's lives positive and fulfilling, rather than withdrawal into a despairing apathy. It *can* be creative and fulfilling work.' But another question has been raised recently: should it always be rehabilitative work? Roger Clough in a recent article in *Social Work Today*, began by quoting another article in *The Guardian* which was entitled 'Elderly Not Ill-treated': ' "Elderly people at an old folk's home, many in their nineties, were made by staff to stagger unaided from meal tables. Sometimes it took them ten minutes to get to their feet. On other occasions they were left on the floor. Yet their treatment did not amount to cruelty. Instead it was part of a deliberate rehabilitation technique to encourage residents to stay active." ' Clough goes on to suggest that rehabilitation, though an acceptable goal in some branches of medicine, may not be appropriate in residential homes for the elderly. There are, he points out, some dilemmas involved:

> Who profits from the treatment? Who decides that it is necessary? As a rule of thumb, treatment régimes should not be imposed on unwilling residents. The power of staff is great and consequently there is a need to guard against thoughtlessly translating their ideas into practice.
>
> I have heard of butter being replaced by margarine ('it's better for their health') and cups of tea available – but only to those who walked to the dining room. Whether these examples are regarded as cruel or not, a resident should have the right to eat butter, even though there are dangers in cholesterol, to remain inactive and lose the use of limbs. After all, males over thirty-five face risks of epidemic proportions from coronary disease, but diets free from salt and daily jogging are not yet compulsory. Like other individuals, the elderly should be able to refuse treatment – and live (or die) with the consequences.

Compulsory care is another matter which causes concern to many. It relates to the move which can be legally forced on people through the operation of Section 47 of the National Assistance Act 1948 and its Amendments of 1951. Many people believe that there is a good case for abolishing this section of the Act altogether. 'Good' GPs have found that time, patience and good social work make it unnecessary in some areas of the country. Others argue that strong-arm methods would have to be used if it were done away with. As it stands, the Act does at least provide a legal safe-guard and proper procedure, which leaves the person concerned with the dignity of having his wishes acknowledged and formally refused, rather than implying that he is mentally incapable by using compulsion under the Mental Health Act, slipping him a sedative or simply telling him that he has no alternative but to comply.

Forcible removal is a traumatic event for anyone however and it raises important, indeed vital, issues about freedom and risk. While the scarcity of long-stay facilities does not encourage casual use of the Act, the present wide and varying interpretation and therefore practice relating to this section give cause for some concern.

There are, of course, many people in institutions who do require rehabilitation and indeed receive it with good effect. Some return to their own homes and often lead lives of a far better quality than those they left upon admission. Dedicated members of staff as well as workers of various organizations and associations contribute to these achievements. Of the latter some have long recognized the urgent need to improve conditions and to extend activities and interest of those spending long periods in homes and hospitals. The British Library of Tape Recordings for Hospital Patients, the British Society for Music Therapy (which promotes the use of music in the treatment of physical as well as emotional and mental disturbances), the organization Paintings in Hospitals, the Council for Music in Hospitals (which brings live concerts of high quality music by professional artists to all kinds of long-stay hospitals and homes throughout Great Britain), are examples; while the Patients' Association exists to represent and further the interests of all patients and will give help and advice to individuals. Any of these organizations can be contacted by individuals, including those responsible for running a hospital or home for elderly residents.

All of us, of course, have a responsibility to ensure that the last days of friends and relations are spent as they themselves wish. Whenever possible this is best achieved in a person's own home. Caring for someone who is dying can be one of the greatest and most privileged experiences of life. It gives us the opportunity to defend their spirit, their sense of dignity and above all, their individuality. The following chapter offers some guidance on how this can be achieved.

CHAPTER 10

CARING FOR SOMEONE WHO IS VERY ILL OR IS DYING

Death opens unknown doors. It is most grand to die.

Pompey the Great I, 'The Chief Centurions'
Man is a Sacred City
John Masefield

Everyone of us, sooner or later, has to come to terms with death: the death of others as well as our own. Attitudes towards the latter will, inevitably, affect the former. Coming to terms with death is a very personal and private happening: perhaps, as Iris Murdoch suggested in one of her earliest novels, 'to accept death is to know God'. It has also been said, 'God gives us love: Something to love He lends us; But when love is grown to ripeness, that on which it throve, falls off; and love is left alone.' How can that love grow to ripeness during out final caring? A period of such caring can be an expression of that love. We will, therefore, want to provide care of the highest standard possible, but how?

As far as we can possibly know, there are three physical expressions of love which most dying people hope for: listening ears, skilled care and companionship until death. According to belief of course, pastoral care should be 'enabled' by the carer.

Listening Ears
The most helpful listener is probably the person who has already thought about, and fully accepted, his or her own death, for he or she will then be aware of the physical loneliness of dying. Despite all the concern, support, compassion and practical help of others, each must experience this last arc of life on this planet alone. An acceptance and an understanding of this unalterable reality can help the listener and in turn, the dying person. (It is stressed that here one is talking about physical alone-ness; implications contained in

146

Psalm 23 and its equivalent in other religions are not forgotten.) Dying people appear quick to sense a warmth, a real concern and the presence of someone who is able to meet them more than half way and is receptive to their expressions (not always verbal) of thought. Only then are they able to feel 'comfortable', to share their feelings, fears, hopes and wishes. False cheerfulness is not helpful and approaching death should never be belittled or made light of.

In the beginning stages, conversation may be somewhat superficial and general, but as confidence in the listener grows, it usually becomes deeper and relevant to the important present situation and experience. A willingness to be *truly present* and to give *completely undivided* attention will create an atmosphere in which the dying person is likely to tell his listener his own understanding of what is happening to him. So there will be no need to wonder, 'Should he be told?'

When someone suspects or knows that his physical condition is serious he or she may wish to talk with a vicar, priest or other spiritual adviser. If the person has none, he or she may wish for one to be called in; usually the earlier such a relationship can be established the more helpful it will be. Part of theological training these days includes service to the sick and dying and in this country, theological students often undertake nursing duties during their training period.

But not everyone practises a religion and no dying person should be made to feel ashamed if he has none. He will undoubtedly have concepts of what he feels to be right or wrong, and if he expresses a disbelief in the existence of a life after death this should be discussed with someone able to meet his need competently.

Skilled Care

Discerning and sensitive physical care is also required during this period. Sometimes this may be given by a member of the family or a friend, supported by the person's own doctor and nurse. The aims of such care will be to provide freedom from fear, freedom from pain, and cleanliness and comfort.

Freedom from fear can only be achieved if one can know or 'sense' the fears. It may be fear of death, of loneliness, of pain, of loss of dignity, of the fate of the family or friends being left, of financial straits anticipated or any other individual and personal anxieties. The first step is to create that atmosphere which will help the dying person to express his fears, for only then can they be dealt with. The 'carer' need not try to do this alone: there are many individuals and organizations who will help, according to the fear expressed. Spiritual advisers, other friends and relations, staff of the social and health services, voluntary agencies – all will give their expertise when and where appropriate. Sometimes very ill people have fears concerning the carer: the nursing is becoming too much, he or she is not getting enough sleep, or the ill person may have fears for the carer after he or she has died. For this reason, the ill person may ask to speak to someone else alone. This should not be resented or taken as a slight, but quietly and efficiently arranged as soon as possible. If there is some truth in the worry that the carer is not getting enough rest this should also be looked into and the doctor or nurse asked to arrange a relief service. In some areas, nursing members of the Red Cross, St John or St Andrew's Association will undertake such duties while the Marie Curie Memorial Foundation will provide a professional day and night nursing service for patients dying from cancer. The National Society for Cancer Relief also provides help, and if transfer to professional care is thought desirable, there are hospices which may be contacted in several large towns throughout the country.

If the fear concerns finance there are many sources of help. In addition to those already outlined, the National Society for Cancer Relief will give financial assistance to help buy special bedding etc. Organizations concerned with specific groups of people such as former doctors (Royal Medical Benevolent Fund), members of the RAF (RAF Benevolent Fund), 'professional and kindred classes' (Royal United Kingdom Beneficient Association) (RUKBA), ex-Officers (Officers' Association); ex-war disabled persons (Order of St John of Jerusalem and the Ex-Services War Disabled Help and Homes Department); Invalids-at-Home, Jewish Aged Needy Pension Society and Guild of Aid for Gentlepeople, will all provide help to those in need, whenever possible.

Freedom from pain is sometimes difficult to achieve, and the control of pain has been a subject of much research in recent years. Major steps forward have been made because of this and unless the pain is an exceptionally difficult nerve pain (intractable pain) it can usually be controlled. Centres which care for dying people have done a good deal of work in this field and will often give advice to GPs. Unfortunately, there is no wonder-drug which works for everyone: one effective for some people may be almost useless or produce unpleasant side effects in others. In order to find out what suits each individual, co-operation between the carer and the doctor and nurses is essential. For this reason it is useful to note and report the ill person's reactions to all medicines and drugs given to him, for only by so doing can the right drug and the effective amount required be ascertained. What has been established by researchers is the time at which a pain-killer should be given and that is *before* the pain sets in. It should therefore be given at regular intervals. Usually this is four-hourly, but the periods may need to be shortened as a tolerance is built up. Nevertheless, the aim should be to allow the dying person to be in control of his dying and to retain his own personality. This *can* be and often is achieved up to the very moment of death.

Until recent years, most people were able to conduct their own dying just as they had been able to conduct their own living. Today, because medical technology has enabled some to become expert in postponing death, we sometimes assume that we have a right to conduct the process of dying for others. Freedom from fear of being 'kept alive' should be available to every dying person.

Cleanliness and comfort depend upon good nursing care. Good preparation for giving nursing care at home is provided by the Red Cross, St John Ambulance and St Andrew's (in Scotland). These three Voluntary Aid Societies give a series of lectures on home nursing and also publish a joint manual *Nursing*. In addition, the Red Cross and St John Ambulance run a short series of four demonstrations during which people can learn and practise how to lift, prevent pressure sores from forming and wash and bath ill people.

Local branches of these societies have lending departments from which can be borrowed many items of nursing equipment such as commodes, back-rests, air cushions, bedpans, bed-cradles, urinals and feeding cups. Members of the domiciliary nursing service in this country will give advice on these and also demonstrate their use. Nursing members of these three Voluntary Aid Societies will also help with nursing care whenever possible. If it is decided that professional nursing is required, the possibility should first be discussed with the district nursing sister of the area in which the patient is living. Private nursing at home is expensive and while there are many good agencies up and down the country, it is wise to take professional advice before contacting any of them.

Food and Drink

The presentation of meals and drinks is important at all times but never more so than when one is caring for someone who is seriously ill. Traycloths and table napkins should be clean and crisp, while only unchipped and uncracked china, sparkling glass and cutlery should be offered. The table napkin should be tucked well under the patient's chin and over the bed-sheet during meals and feeds: dropped food or spilt liquid can cause great distress as well as additional laundry.

The diet of a dying person need not be restricted but usually meals are best tolerated if they are small and frequent. It may be easier for the ill person to take food which has been liquidized or puréed. Lack of food will cause a feeling of distressing tiredness and frequent small feeds can prevent this. Glucose, although more expensive than sugar, is quickly turned to energy and may be sprinkled on fruit and puddings. Nourishing drinks may also be given but if they contain milk, the mouth should be rinsed afterwards to keep it clean and fresh.

Egg-nog is quite a favourite, especially if a few spoonfuls of brandy are added. Colour and decorations should also be used but with discretion. Milk puddings can be 'decorated' with grated nutmeg, soups with chopped parsley, ice-cream with half a glacé cherry or nut and fruit drinks with a half-slice of orange, lime or lemon. Even if these decorations cannot be eaten, the sight of them is likely to give a little pleasure.

Feeding someone who is very ill is an art to be learned. If it becomes necessary, ask a member of the nursing service or an experienced Red Cross, St John or St Andrew's nursing member to demonstrate this skill. The former will also be able to advise on, for example, special cutlery, feeders, angled feeding-straws, all of which will help to make feeding less stressful to both the carer and the ill person.

In order to prevent unnecessary discomfort, all body systems should be encouraged to function as normally as possible. Adequate diet of the right *kind* of foods can help here. For example, fruit and vegetables (liquidized or puréed if necessary) will help to prevent constipation, while an adequate intake of fluids will help to keep the kidneys working well and help to prevent infection of the urine which often causes frequency or even incontinence (loss of control of passing urine).

Fruit juice or water, or both, should be left within reach of the ill person and a thermos of hot milk or other favourite beverage should be at hand for the night.

Needless to say, this depends upon the condition of the patient: if there is any likelihood of an accident, hot fluid should not be left within reach, and constant attendance, including help with the taking of all drinks, may be necessary as death approches. Sometimes sucking a boiled sweet or chewing a piece of chewing gum helps to keep the patient's mouth and tongue moist but there is a danger of choking if he is not fully alert. Frequent mouthwashes will also help to keep the mouth moist.

If alcohol is usually taken before, during, or after meals there is no reason why the habit should not be continued during illness if so desired, providing it is not incompatible with any medicine or pain-killer being given.

Nausea can often be relieved by a little soda water, or warm water in which a pinch of sodium bicarbonate has been dissolved or tonic water. (All incidentally can also be used as mouth-rinses.)

Indigestion may be relieved by sucking one of the brand tablets on the market or taking mixtures sold by chemists for dyspepsia or by sipping a little peppermint water (*aqua. menth. pip.* which is sold by most pharmacies) to which a little hot water has been added. A crushed charcoal biscuit in brandy sometimes helps to dispel any wind which is causing discomfort.

The vomiting of food and fluids can be a distressing part of some illnesses but there are several medicines to prevent this from happening and the GP will be able to prescribe one. When someone is being sick, support his forehead with one hand, while holding a bowl for him to be sick into with the other. When a vomiting attack is over, give a warm mouthwash (several pleasant-tasting ones are available) and sponge the ill person's face and mouth with warm water. Dry gently but thoroughly. If the bed linen or clothing has been soiled, change it immediately. The sense of smell is especially acute when the body is sick and it is important to remove the source of smells such as vomit, as well as to prevent other smells such as those from the kitchen, from permeating the sick room. Smells which may be hardly noticeable to others can be a source of great distress to a very ill person.

Grooming

Concepts of cleanliness vary, but the person's standards should not be lowered because he or she is dying.

Washing and bathing should be frequent enough to give the ill person the feeling and appearance of cleanliness, to control body odours, and to protect the skin from laceration and other forms of irritation. The normal hairstyle should be continued and *not* a new one adopted because it would be easier to manage (such as plaits or 'bunches' for a woman, or a shorter cut for a man).

Incontinence

Sometimes, a loss of control of the bladder and bowel causes great distress. Incontinence of urine can often be prevented by giving a bedpan or urinal at regular two-hourly intervals. There are several shapes and sizes available and the district nursing sister will give advice about suitability and which can be borrowed from the local branch of the Red Cross or St John Ambulance. Regular bowel actions can sometimes be achieved by ensuring that the diet contains roughage or bulk (the bulky cereals are quite good). If bran cannot be eaten, there are several 'bulk agents' which can be prescribed by the doctor. Diarrhoea (if not caused by an 'overflow' from constipation), can often be controlled by giving a dissolved soluble codein tablet in a little brandy, while constipation may sometimes be remedied by giving milk of magnesia or paraffin emulsion. As the latter is rather oily it can be made more palatable by mixing it with a little fruit juice. Clean, wash and dry the ill person gently but thoroughly after each bowel action, to keep the skin comfortable and free from sores.

If incontinence of urine or faeces (stools) does occur, the soiled bed and other clothing should be changed, the ill person's skin washed with soap and water, and dried gently but thoroughly. A barrier skin cream can be used to prevent the skin from becoming soggy and sore.

When incontinence is inevitable ask the domiciliary nursing sister what aids and services are available in the area: whether the authority supplies personal equipment such as pants, pads, urinals and bedpans; whether the local authority provides a laundry service to collect and clean dirty linen and clothing, and whether the local authority collects soiled pads or provides special bags so that they can be collected with normal refuse.

Urinals

These are receptacles into which urine can be passed. A urinal can be kept nearby and is very useful if it can be managed independently and without spilling. This equipment can be bought at or ordered from many large chemists or surgical suppliers.

i) *Male urinals (bottles):* there are many different makes, some in lightweight plastic (polypropylene) and others in stainless steel. Plastic or stainless steel urinals are available from many places including A. C. Daniels and Downs Surgical Ltd. (For full list of suppliers see ISD List No. 7A – Personal Toilet available from the Disabled Living Foundation).

ii) *A non-spill adaptor:* Made of rigid nylon with a rubber sleeve, this will fit most male urinals and is very useful in preventing spilling if the user is in bed or chair. It is available in packs of five from Charles F. Thackray Ltd.

iii) *The Reddy-Bottle:* a disposable male urine collector which has a built-in non-return valve. Enquiries should be made to Downs Surgical Ltd.

Female urinals:

Apart from the standard bedpans used in hospitals, there are several types of urinals especially designed for women. As with male urinals, some are in plastic and some in stainless steel.

i) *St. Peters Boat:* a pointed plastic dish with handle which can be slipped easily between the legs and can be used while standing, it is made by Cape and is available through A. W. Gregory & Co. Ltd.

ii) *Suba-Seal Female pan type urinal:* a small shallow non-spill plastic dish with a capped hollow handle (through which it is emptied) which can easily be slipped under the buttocks when the user is lying or sitting. It does not involve raising the hips. It is made by William Freeman & Co. Ltd.

iii) *The Feminal:* a handbag size personal urinal with a lightweight plastic frame contoured to fit female anatomy and supports a disposable plastic bag. it is held in position for use by front handle and can be used sitting, lying or standing. It is made by Searle Medical, and is available through Medimail.

Incontinence appliances should be well and frequently cleaned. Both smell and crystalline deposit can be prevented by daily cleaning. It is an advantage to have two appliances so that one can be cleaned and allowed to dry before re-use. A dry appliance is more comfortable for the wearer and the material is better preserved when dried after washing. Warm water and a special antiseptic compound such as Savlon liquid or Dettol can be used for cleaning most appliances. Solutions such as Milton (sodium hypochlorite) are very effective germicides. In diluted form they may be used for cleaning plastic urinal bottles and most other plastic appliances. Rubber appliances are, however, damaged by hypochlorite solutions and a weak solution of one of the antiseptics such as Dettol should be used; a very strong solution of ordinary salt, which has antiseptic properties is also good and should be left in the appliance for half an hour or so. Oils, cleaning fluids, hard soap or strong detergents can adversely affect rubber; if in doubt, advice on the care of appliances can be obtained from the manufacturer. Products mentioned above may be obtained through chemists and all should be used according to the makers' instructions.

Good ventilation, a little disinfectant (e.g. Dettol) in household cleaning water, and a good supply of underclothes and protective pants to allow for frequent changing into clean garments are all important factors in maintaining freshness.

Pads and Pants

If plastic and proofed-nylon pants are found to be hot and uncomfortable, Kanga pants may provide a solution. These are made of soft one-way fabric which allows the urine to pass through and absorbed by a special Kanga pad which is held in a plastic pouch on the outside of the garment. This can be changed without removing the pants. More comprehensive and up-to-date information on these and other forms of protection is given in the List 12 available from the Information Service of the Disabled Living Foundation.

An alternative is to use cellulose wadding, which is supplied in rolls, and can be cut to make pads of the desired size and thickness. Some types are thicker or wider than others, and some have waterproof backing. This is obtainable from chemists on NHS prescription.

Mattress protection

There are various types of mattress protectors; the Sandra range, made in both heavy duty and lightweight plastic, includes drawsheets, box-style covers to envelop the mattress completely, and covers which protect top and sides with either fitted corners or tapes. All are obtainable from Home Nursing Supplies and these and other makes are also available through chemists. The domiciliary nursing sister may also be able to provide requirements of this kind.

Bedpads

Disposable bedpads can be used to absorb urine. These will probably be supplied through the domiciliary nurse and some pads are more absorbent than others. The domiciliary nurse's advice should be sought if the kind provided does not prove satisfactory. The pad should be placed under the buttocks *across* the bed, not lengthwise. One of the most absorbent is the Polyweb, obtainable through local chemists, and sometimes supplied through the local nursing staff. A useful aid in keeping the incontinent person dry and comfortable is the Marathon Dri-sheet. This is a draw sheet obtainable in two sizes – 33″ × 33″ or 33″ × 17″ – made of knitted one-way fabric which allows moisture to pass through and be absorbed by a bed pad or other absorptive padding underneath; the sheet itself, and the body of the user, remain dry, provided the padding is changed regularly. Supplies may be obtained through local chemists or from J. H. Bounds Ltd.

One way of making up the bed might be:
   i) Some form of waterproof covering over the mattress.
  ii) A bottom sheet; nylon are very easily laundered, but some people find them hot.
 iii) A draw sheet of lightweight plastic, about one metre by two, across the bed.
  iv) A bedpad or other absorbent padding.
   v) A Marathon Dri-sheet.

If there is a heavy loss of urine, or more especially if there is double incontinence, the wearing of a disposable combined pad-and-pant may be advisable, e.g. Cumfies or Molnlycke, as described on page 127.

Kylie Absorbent Bed Sheet

This new type of bed protection has recently become available. The Kylie is a highly absorbent padded drawsheet and is washable. It eliminates the need for an underpad and even after some hours of use the surface remains relatively dry and comfortable. It is available from Nicholas Laboratories Ltd.

Laundry

The following suggestions may be helpful for those concerned with laundry for an incontinent person at home.
   i) The two major problems are smell and staining, particularly when urine or faeces are left on articles exposed to the air so that bacterial decomposition takes place. If possible, wet or soiled clothing or bed linen should be removed immediately, rinsed out and soaked in cold water in a covered bucket. 'Napisan' can be added to help cleanse. The article can then be washed in the usual way and no staining will result. Some people use biological washing powders, but this should not be necessary when rinsing and soaking are carried out immediately; these powders are strong and may cause irritation to the skin.
  ii) If laundry is not possible at home, advice and help should be sought from the domiciliary nurse or health visitor. In certain areas there is a special laundry service run by the local health authority or social services

department where collection may take place once or twice a week, and where bags are supplied for the soiled articles.

iii) There are also disposable pads to be worn with protective pants, disposable bedpads, and combined protective pant-and-pad garments which are completely disposable. Both items are suitable for urinary and faecal incontinence.

Odour Control

Problems of odour arise when urine or faeces are exposed to the air. The following suggestions may be helpful:

i) It is essential to deal with any wet or soiled articles as speedily as possible. Disposable padding should be rolled up and wrapped in newspaper or small plastic bags and placed immediately in a container with a lid; a bucket or bin lined with a polythene bag which can be closed securely and removed when full is a good idea. Wet or soiled clothing or bed linen should be removed and dealt with as soon as possible.

ii) There are neutralising deodorants which help to eliminate odour. One example is Nilodor, which is inexpensive and obtainable from large chemists or direct from Loxley Medical Supplies Ltd. A drop or two can be used in appliances, commode pans, urinals, bedpans and on protective padding. A few drops can be added to the water used for washing commodes, carpets, etc.

iii) Personal cleanliness is obviously important – ordinary soap and water is quite adequate, though some people prefer a bactericidal soap such as Cidal. When protective padding is used it should be changed frequently, and a small amount of barrier cream may be used to help prevent soreness (e.g. Vasogen or Kerodex Double Seven available on prescription). Talcum powder is not always a good idea as it tends to form into lumps when wet and then holds urine close to the skin; if powder is used it should be applied very lightly.

Sleep

Before settling an ill person for the night, he or she should always be offered a bedpan or urinal (or, of course, accom-

panied to the w.c. if that is possible). The person is likely to
be very reluctant to disturb the sleep of the carer and may
even spend distressful hours rather than do so.

His or her position in bed is also important and much
trouble and time may be needed to discover which is the most
comfortable. Usually it is the one in which the individual
leans back on three or four pillows with knees slightly flexed.
Whichever position is adopted, it should be one which allows
movement of limbs and lets the body organs function as
normally as possible.

If a dying person becomes unconscious, he should be gently
turned onto one side with his body almost prone, one flexed
arm in front and the other lying beside and behind his body.
To give stability the upper leg should be slightly flexed also.

Surprising though it may sound, pressure sores can cause
discomfort even at this stage so the regular treatment of
pressure areas should be continued. This includes regular
changes of position. Healthy people move constantly, even in
sleep; and those who are unable to move themselves must be
carefully moved by others. Professional nurses will demonstrate this and will also show families or friends how to carry
out other procedures to prevent pressure sores from forming.

A dying person is often cold. Duvets or continental quilts
are lighter than blankets and if available, may be preferred,
as the latter tend to limit the circulation of the blood thereby
increasing the cold feeling. If bedwarmers are used, great care
must be taken: a hot water bottle should be well protected
with a cover and placed between two blankets, not directly
close to the person. Electric pads and blankets should be used
according to precautions outlined in the manufacturer's instructions. There are several good ones on the market which
can be left on all night even when the individual is incontinent. Bedsocks, mittens, bedjackets and shawls are all recommended and extra covering should be left within reach for the
cooler hours of early morning. If a window is left open, a
screen (or an improvised screen made by draping a blanket
over a clothes horse) should protect the patient from draughts.
If, however, he is too hot, a bed-cradle (borrowed from the
Red Cross, St John or St Andrew's), will allow air to circulate
more freely. A small electric fan can also be useful.

Most people sleep better in the dark, so if it is necessary to
leave a light on in order to observe the ill person better, it

should be shaded by a cloth or a duster draped and knotted over the lampshade, but kept well away from the bulb. During the day, if curtains and blinds are inadequate or make the room too stuffy, an eye-shade can be made from soft material using the pattern of those issued by some air-lines on long distance flights. Such a shade is also useful at night if there is a bothersome street light or the observation light is too bright even when shaded.

Noisy doors, rattling windows, dripping taps and clicking central heating can all prevent sleep. If the noise is uncontrollable (traffic for example), malleable wax ear plugs (obtainable from most chemists), or small plugs of cotton wool may be useful.

If discomfort comes from excessive sweating, warm sponging and drying all over (in the same way as one carries out a bed-bath), followed by a complete change of night clothes and bed linen, will often bring some relief and pleasure. Discomfort can also be caused by a rucked undersheet, the weight of bed-clothes, a soiled dressing or a skin irritation. All have obvious remedies.

Breathing

Sometimes very ill people experience breathlessness which may be caused by a variety of reasons.

To be breathless is a very frightening experience. Most of us have experienced first hand the frightening effect of choking when we have caught our breath or 'swallowed the wrong way'. We know the near-panic which can result and it is helpful to remember this near-panic when caring for a breathless person. Reassurance and a calm presence are vital which can only be given if one knows what to do and how to do it.

The person may find it easier to breathe propped up in a sitting position, in which case his head, neck and back will need supporting by a back-rest and several firm but comfortable pillows (with no spaces between them). A footrest, made from wrapping a pillow in an old sheet, twisting the ends and tucking them under the mattress, will help the person to maintain this position. It may take some time to find a comfortable one. Even in hospital, with professional expertise and specially designed beds, it is not easy. Skill, time, knowledge, patience and confidence will all be needed, but a generous expenditure of all these will prove worthwhile.

When breathing is particularly difficult or painful, the breathing muscles are continuously in action which can be tiring and distressing. Easier movement can be obtained by 'fixing' the shoulder muscles, which can be done by helping the individual to lean forward on to a bedtable (or a table alongside the bed with the person sitting over the side, facing it), supporting the body with his or her *elbows* resting on the table. In some instances, severe breathlessness is accompanied by involuntary nodding movements of the head, and a headrest upon which the ill person may lay his or her forehead will reduce the discomfort. An air, rubber or foam ring to sit on will ease the inevitable pressure this position will put on the buttocks. All can be borrowed or hired from a local depot of one of the three Voluntary Aid Societies referred to earlier.

Sometimes a patient who becomes breathless finds that he is more comfortable sitting in an armchair instead of a bed. If this is so, the legs and feet should be raised on to another chair at intervals in order to prevent swelling of the ankles and feet. But whatever position is taken the person will inevitably need help to move again because breathless people are restless people.

Prevention of breathlessness is important and because a change in room temperature can stimulate a bout of breathlessness, this should be kept fairly constant. It is also useful to note any food which causes an attack so that it can be avoided in the future. Usually, it is the hard, dry foods which irritate and the soft, moist and easily digested ones which soothe. When feeding is necessary, give only a very small mouthful at a time because chewing and swallowing are especially difficult when one is having difficulty in breathing.

Dry, irritating coughs can sometimes be suppressed by sipping water, sucking a boiled sweet or by taking a little prescribed linctus. A productive cough (one which results in the expectoration of sputum) should be encouraged on the other hand, because getting rid of the sputum will help to relieve the discomfort. Sometimes it may be necessary to remove sputum which has been coughed into the mouth. This should be done gently with the fingers protected by a clean piece of rag (paper tissues disintegrate unless they are the very thick, tough variety). Rag used for this purpose should be burnt and all tissues flushed down the w.c.

When breathing has to be through the mouth, the lips and tongue can become very dry. Frequent sips of water or fruit juice should be given (a cup or mug is easier to manipulate than a glass). Lip salve, available from a chemist, will soothe any flaking lips, while a bland cream should be smeared around the nostrils to prevent crusts from forming.

Sometimes it is necessary to clean the teeth and mouth of a very ill patient for him. This is another procedure which a nurse will demonstrate.

Companionship

It is extremely important for someone to *be* with a dying person: to touch, hold and speak to him as well as to listen and carry out his wishes. Those whom the person wants should be asked to attend and then left alone. If the patient expresses a wish to see a spiritual adviser he also should be sent for, no matter what the time of day and night. It is important not to wait until death is imminent for then the patient cannot co-operate. When asking a minister or priest to call, it is helpful to tell him whether the dying person is conscious or not, whether he is able to swallow or not and whether he is being sick. Only then can the priest judge the form his visit will take. If an unconscious patient regains consciousness, the minister, priest or other adviser may wish to pay another visit before a further lapse occurs. When a person dies, his spiritual adviser should be informed.

Some people remain conscious until death, while others become unconscious several hours or even days before. It is important to remember that unconscious people can often hear because hearing is the last of our senses to leave us. Sight and speech may deteriorate gradually. When this happens it is even more important to touch and speak to the ill person so that the person knows he or she is not alone. If wishes or discomforts cannot be expressed, every effort should be made to anticipate them. The carer should plump up a lumpy, hot pillow, move the patient's head if it involuntarily falls into an uncomfortable position, moisten the person's lips and mouth if swallowing is difficult, sponge and dry sweating skin, change any soiled linen, alter the patient's position to prevent 'pins and needles', and so on. The presence of pets to stroke or the smell of favourite flowers should not be forgotten, for all can give pleasure during those last precious hours. Obviously, one must use discretion and knowledge of the person involved but it should be borne in mind that for some people 'companionship', indeed 'religion', can mean music and readings from special books, plays and poetry. Likewise, until sight is lost, favourite pictures, photographs, prized possessions or trophies should be placed within sight. All such wishes will be individual and can only be anticipated by someone who knows and loves to that full ripeness.

Even when a dying person cannot answer and he or she appears to be completely unconscious, continue to speak to that person, reassuring, comforting and loving until death comes. And when he is in such complete and final dependence, continue to protect the person from loss of dignity so that he or she may conduct his or her own dying, *enabled* to do so by you. In this extreme situation we will all have to depend upon others to defend our most precious possessions – our spirit, our sense of dignity and, above all our individuality. The least we can do is to provide that defence for others.

CHAPTER 11

BEING PRACTICAL WHEN BEREAVED

Knowledge by suffering entereth;
And Life is perfected by Death.

'A Vision of Poets'
Elizabeth Barrett Browning 1806–1861

Death is a logical sequence to ageing. Yet, while man is defined as 'the only animal who can think about what is not there', he seems to find death a difficult subject to contemplate.

Partly because of increasing secularism over recent decades, a number of people have relegated their own deaths to the background of consciousness. Many are not prepared for it and others try to deny its existence. Among professional carers and curers there are those who challenge death as a larger event than their own puny effort to keep people alive. Sometimes one is reminded of the description of the life of one of Aldous Huxley's characters in *Brief Candles*. 'It was not really a life at all. It was just galvanic activity like the twitching of a dead frog's legs when you touch the nerve with an electrified wire.'

We are surrounded by evidence of death in our everyday lives: the butcher's shop, the fly in the spider's web, the bird on the motorway, the leaves of Autumn. Yet, as Lewis Thomas writes:

It is always a queer shock, part a sudden upwelling of grief, part unaccountable amazement. It is simply astounding to see an animal dead on a highway. The outrage is more than just the location, it is the impropriety of such *visible* death, anywhere . . . It is the nature of animals to die alone, off somewhere, hidden. It is wrong to see them lying out in the highway; it is wrong to see them anywhere. . . Whoever sees dead birds in anything like the large numbers stipulated by the certainty of the death of all birds?. . . Animals seem to have an instinct for performing death alone, hidden. . . If an elephant mis-steps and dies in an open place, the herd will not leave him there; the others will pick him up and carry the body from place to place, finally putting it down in some inexplicably suitable location . . . it is a natural marvel.

There are three billion of us on earth, and all three billion must be dead, on a schedule, within a lifetime. This vast mortality involves over fifty million of us each year. To quote Lewis Thomas again, 'Less than a half century from now, our replacements will have more than doubled the numbers. . . . We will have to give up the notion that death is catastrophic or detestable, or avoidable, or even strange.

We are brought up, of course, with the instinctive animal fear of death and with strong instincts of preservation and procreation. Throughout history, death has been something terrible: capital punishment is the greatest price a criminal is asked to pay, we fight until death and we love until death. Our art depicts sad scenes of death and dying, and our literature is full of tragic inconsolable, tormented and tortured dying and bereaved figures. Even the psalmists write of the valley of death, darkness and the shadow of death. Both Wetherell and Lyndhurst speak of 'other' or 'new' terrors of death. And Shakespeare writes of 'bosom black as death', although he, more than most dramatists, accepted death. There is Hamlet's famous speech:

> Whether 'tis nobler in the mind to suffer
> The slings and arrows of outrageous fortune,
> Or to take arms against a sea of troubles,
> And by opposing end them? To die; to sleep;
> No more; and by a sleep to say we end
> The heartache and the thousand natural shocks
> That flesh is heir to? – 'tis a consummation
> Devoutly to be wished. To die, to sleep;
> To sleep, perchance to dream, ay, there's the rub;
> For in that sleep of death what dreams may come,
> When we have shuffled off this mortal coil,
> Must give us pause:

Again, Caesar in *Julius Caesar* answers Calpurnia's comment:

> Cowards die many times before their deaths;

The valiant never taste of death but once.
Of all the wonders that I yet have heard,
it seems to be most strange that men should fear;
Seeing that death, a necessary end, will come when it will
come.

Many psychoanalysts believe that everyone carries in their
mind a basic anxiety about death. This, in our society, is
hardly surprising, considering how many of us are brought
up to view it through our readings, pictures and indeed our
whole culture.

Death is often treated as a taboo subject even now, when
sex and money and other previously taboo subjects have been
'exorcised' as Michael Gaine calls it. Yet death is the most
important event in our lives and surely development of the
spirit is the best preparation for it? The form that preparation
takes is an individual decision; often it is also a private one.

In *Learning to Grow Old*, Paul Tournier writes about the
problems of facing up to death. He suggests that over the
centuries the Churches have exploited the fear men feel when
they are confronted with death. Certainly some 'believers'
appear to be more shocked and less accepting of the deaths
of friends and relations than some 'non-believers'. Georges
Bernanos, in his *Dialogue des Carmelites*, describes how even
the strongly religious Sister Blanche, with her great qualities
of strength and piety, finds it so hard to die. The 'Four Last
Things' (death, judgement, heaven and hell) have been used
for centuries as a system of reward and punishment and as
a form of conditioning individual moral and spiritual responses. Although the tradition of hell-fire sermons during
missions and revivalist meetings is for the most part a thing
of the past, today's old people may well have been brought
up on them.

With the 'judgement and punishment' doctrine from the
Christian Church and the lack of an alternative afterlife from
the humanists it is little wonder that some people have turned
to Eastern religions and others have been left with little idea
of how to prepare themselves, and others for death. But as
Tournier writes, 'Death is indeed the moment of truth which
upsets all our vain categories. It is only our preconceived
notions which are surprised by unexpected, but quite natural
reactions.'

It has been shown that belief in an after-life increases dramatically in older age groups. Whether this is due to ageing or simply reflects that the older generation have greater certainty about traditional beliefs, is not known. Michael Argyle and B. Beit-Hallahmi write, 'The heightened religion of age is very different from the heightened religion of adolescence. In adolescence, there is a great intellectual perplexity and doubt, coupled with emotional turmoil; young people suddenly change their whole orientation one way or the other. In old age, when both intellect and emotions are dimmed, there is no worry about the niceties of theology, nor is there any emotional excitement about religious matters.'

But at any age when confronted with death in the form of the death of a loved one we often feel 'numb with grief'. For married people the loss of a husband or wife can be literally devastating. This may include overwhelming feelings of isolation, guilt or even anger at being left. Each of us also experiences something different and unique when a parent dies. Because we consider ourselves as an extension of our parents we lose our own sense of immortality at such a time.

Sleep brings some respite from grief but with each awaking comes the realization anew. The realization dawns that friend, husband, wife or parent is not there to join in the day's activities, to talk about what is in the newspapers, to share jokes, to be infuriating and to give confidence and a feeling of purpose: in short, to share our lives.

Grieving at this time is normal and should not be denied: sedation will only postpone, not remove it. Activity can help and while no immediate major decisions concerning the future should be made by an elderly bereaved spouse, immediate action concerned with one's statutory responsibilities and with personal arrangements for funeral, burial or cremation can be actually helpful.

Statutory Responsibilities

If the GP was not present at the time of death, he must be informed. He will certify death and issue the death certificate. This should be taken to the registrar's office and the death registered there.

If there are any unusual circumstances the death will be reported to the coroner or appropriate authority. (A coroner is a qualified doctor or lawyer and sometimes both. He is appointed by the County or County Borough Council, but is responsible to the Crown only.) He will then decide if a death certificate can be issued, or whether it is desirable to arrange for a post-mortem examination. If the coroner wishes to hold an inquest, the certificate of death cannot be issued by the doctor until this has taken place.

Medical Certificate of Death

As the law of this country requires that every death shall be registered, medical evidence of the cause of death must be given either by the family doctor or by the doctor who looked after the person during his final illness, and by a coroner. The doctor is legally bound to issue a medical certificate stating the cause of death even when there is uncertainty about the precise diagnosis, in which case he or she will state the cause of death 'to the best of [his] knowledge and belief'. The doctor also gives the last date on which he or she saw the patient alive and states whether or not another doctor has also seen the body. No charge is made for this certificate.

When a death has been reported to the coroner, the registrar must wait until the coroner advises him that he is authorized to register the death. Reporting a death to the coroner does not inevitably mean an inquest or a post-mortem examination, although the majority of deaths reported to the coroner do lead to the latter and some to the former. It is up to each individual coroner to decide what action is to be taken.

A Post-mortem Examination

If the coroner orders a post-mortem examination, no appeal can be made against the decision. The coroner's office becomes responsible for the body and removes it to the mortuary. After the examination has been carried out, the body once more becomes the responsibility of the family, unless there is to be an inquest.

In most districts the coroner's office (or a policeman) will inform the family or friend of the results of the post-mortem examination, but it is not their duty to do so and in some areas the next-of-kin (or the undertaker) will need to enquire at the registrar's office.

An Inquest

Whereas a post-mortem examination is carried out to establish the physical cause of death, an inquest is held to establish who the deceased was, and when and where he died. An inquest is held whenever there are reasonable grounds for suspecting the death was due to un-natural causes or followed an accident. It does not involve the family or friends in any expense unless they employ a solicitor. This is advisable if death was the result of an accident or of an occupational disease, as help may be required in order to make appropriate claims. People who do not have a solicitor can obtain advice at the local Citizens Advice Bureau. After the inquest, the coroner sends a certificate to the registrar and the death can then be registered.

Registering a Death

In this country a death should be registered within five days of its occurrence. Registration can be delayed for a further nine days in special circumstances, but only if the Registrar receives full particulars in writing, including medical evidence of the cause of death.

Under English law, a death must be registered in the district in which it has occurred. A list of names, addresses and telephone numbers of local registrars is usually displayed in post offices, public libraries and in some doctors' surgeries. It is well to note the hours the office is open as some are not open during all normal office hours. The procedure of registration takes the form of a question-and-answer interview. First the registrar will establish that the death took place in his own sub-district as he may not register a death which has occurred outside his area of jurisdiction. He will also want to know the relationship of the informant to the deceased. A draft form will then be filled in with details of the informant, the date on which the death took place, the address at which it occurred and the name and sex of the person. The names given should include *all* those by which the deceased was ever known and *all* those on birth and marriage certificates as well as on all other official or relevant documents. This will avoid any future difficulties relating to such issues as insurance policies, probate and bank accounts etc. When a person dies away from home, his own home address should also be given. The precise occupation of the deceased will also be asked: it is not enough to give 'businessman' or 'traveller'. The profession or occupation of a wife or widow at the time of her death must also be recorded and in addition, she should be described as 'the wife of' or 'the widow of'. An unmarried woman should have her profession or occupation described and her marital status given.

The informant should check very carefully this draft of the proposed entry as after it has been signed, alterations and amendments can be made only with the authority of the Registrar General. The next-of-kin will be asked to endorse with his or her signature the information given to the registrar. This has to be done in special ink, so the registrar's pen, not one's own, must be used. After the signing the registrar will issue copies of the entry, which will be needed for official purposes such as probate. In case further copies are required at a future date, a note should be made at this point of the number of the entry, the date, the registrar and the registration district. The registrar will also ask for the dead person's pension book, medical card and any allowance order books. Again, it is wise to make a note of the numbers of all these before handing them over to him as the information may well be needed for other purposes later.

Funeral Arrangements

In the United Kingdom bodies are either buried or cremated. If cremation is to take place, four additional forms have to be completed. This is standard procedure and no exception is made.

At this point it is usual to ask a funeral director (or undertaker) to take over arrangements. While he will be as helpful and considerate as possible, he must be given some information regarding wishes for the funeral. He will need to know whether the body is to be embalmed, the type of shroud, coffin and coffin-lining to be used, the name of the chosen church, cemetery or crematorium and how many mourning motor-cars will be required. Funerals can be costly and it is wise to ask for a written quotation of expenses, as the 'extras' to what is known as 'the respectable basics' can be considerable. A sensible decision should be arrived at, bearing in mind the possible future expenses of a headstone if burial is to take place, or a rose-tree or some other floral memorial if cremation has been decided on. Fees of the grave digger, clergyman, organist and choir are usually paid in advance by the undertaker who then includes the total in his account. To help defray the cost of a funeral, a death grant may be applied for.

A Death Grant

There are two levels of death grant and while neither is large enough to cover the total cost of a funeral, both can be a help towards meeting expenses.

To claim the death grant, the death certificate, the deceased's marriage certificate and the written estimate of funeral expenses should be presented to the local social security office (the address will be in the local telephone directory). The grant is paid on the national insurance contributions of the deceased or on those of the widow or widower and is made to whomsoever is responsible for the funeral expenses.

If the deceased was seventy-seven years old (if a woman) or eighty-two years old (if a man) *before* July 5th 1975 only a reduced grant will be made. If the deceased was eighty-seven years old (if a woman) or ninety-two years old (if a man) *before* July 5th 1975 no grant will be given. But for those who receive supplementary benefits, help with funeral expenses can be obtained through the local social security office. If a funeral cannot be afforded the local authority may arrange a simple one and claim the death grant themselves.

What to do When Someone Dies published by the Consumer Association gives further details regarding all aspects of the subject while a leaflet, 'The Death Grant', obtainable from local social security offices provides more information on this specific form of financial help.

After the Funeral

After the burial or cremation there will be other matters to see to such as probate, insurance, the deceased person's bank account, post office account, and so on. If help is required, the local branch of Age Concern or the local Citizens Advice Bureau may give it.

Probably the most painful activity (and one which probably should involve at least two people at a time), is the sorting out of clothes, possessions, papers and letters of the dead person. This can cause great distress as even parting with a

toothbrush or a pair of shoes can seem like treachery. There
is a great desire to keep physical and tangible evidence of the
loved one, a desire deeply indulged by Queen Victoria all her
life after the death of the Prince Consort.

It is at this stage too that one can experience auditory or
visual hallucinations: that is, one hears the voice of, or sees
the dead person. It is said by psychologists that these represent a sub-conscious rejection of the death, although there are
some people who believe otherwise. For some, these voices
and appearances can bring great comfort for they feel that
the dead person is with them again and that they can talk
and share some aspects of life once more. For others they can
cause fear and particularly fear of insanity. It is important to
realize that this is just one stage of grieving and that most
people who have loved a person very deeply, pass through it.
Sometimes it gives way to a feeling of guilt: one thinks one
could and should have done so much more. It is at this stage
that some widows and widowers experience depression, often
at a suicidal level, and both spiritual and medical advisers
should be requested to help.

Unfortunately, our traditional customs relating to death
and bereaved people have been gradually eroded over recent
years. In the past, the following of a ritualized pattern of
behaviour often helped people to cope with this particular
personal tragedy. Now, the subject of a recent death is often
ignored very quickly by family and friends, and the old person
is 'jollied' along and told 'not to dwell on it'. This often means
that he is left bewildered and isolated in his grief and is not
able to work through all those stages of bereavement which
are necessary if he is to accept it and adjust.

Bereavement frequently either strengthens faith or threatens it. It has been found that elderly people living at home
often find it easier to adjust than those in institutions. Faith
can play a part in this adjustment, as it can in other personal
crises such as retirement.

Obviously, feelings of frustration, fear and even anger have
to be expressed and these emotions worked through. Sometimes, for fear of shocking their families and friends they are
repressed and the husband or wife left alone may 'withdraw'
from the activities of this world, sit alone thinking and reliving
a more secure and happier past. Bereaved people frequently
suffer from insomnia and have disturbed nights. They often

lose weight and their usual leisure activities are abandoned. At this stage, well-meaning sons or daughters may feel it is their duty to move their parent left alone to live with them. *Such action needs very careful thought and full discussion by all concerned before being implemented.*

For the majority of people, the first six months after bereavement are the worst. After one year, most will be picking up threads of an individual life once more. If this is not happening, spiritual and medical help should be sought again.

The last step is when the dying, the death and the grief has been accepted, interpreted and absorbed into one's life: this 'firing' process brings about changes in one's personality and they can be for the good. All experiences in life of course can be used in this way to develop 'self', but bereavement can be one of the most influential. There are many helpful books written on mourning and grieving. In addition, or as an alternative, there are one or two organizations who will help. CRUSE provides a counselling service offering understanding, practical advice and encouragement to widows and widowers and their children. There is also the National Association of Widows, the Widows' Association of Great Britain and the Widows' Friend Society, while the National Council for the Single Woman and Her Dependants will help a single person who wants assistance with planning life after the death of a parent.

It is when this latter stage has been reached that more permanent arrangements can be made for future living. Housing and financial status will influence all such decisions, but every possibility and alternative should be carefully thought through, considered and discussed, before definite plans are formed. Picking up old interests and mutual friends, as well as making new contacts, may not be easy but will be of great value in helping one back to live life again, for as T. S. Eliot writes in *Four Quartets*:

Time present and time past
Are both perhaps present in time future,
And time future contained in time past.

APPENDIX I

SOURCES OF GENERAL INFORMATION RELATING TO ELDERLY PEOPLE AND SOME ORGANIZATIONS AND TRUSTS WHICH GIVE HELP IN SPECIFIC INSTANCES

I only ask for information.

David Copperfield
Charles Dickens 1812–1870

HOUSING

All local authorities will have names of homes within their area and Counsel and Care for the Elderly will also be able to supply information.

For further information on housing, the following may be consulted:

Housing Advice Centres
Most are listed in the telephone directory under the name of the borough council in which they are located. They provide information free of charge. The Citizens Advice Bureau will also have a list of them.

Citizens Advice Bureaux
Addresses of local bureaux will be found in the local telephone directory.

Local Housing Authority Departments
Addresses will be listed in the telephone directory under the name of the borough Council.

Department of the Environment
The D.O.E. (or Scottish Development Department (S.D.D.) in Scotland) is the government department responsible for housing policy in both the public and private sectors. It issues free information pamphlets from: Building 3, Victoria Road, South Ruislip Middx. Their leaflets can also be obtained from the housing advice centres and from the Citizens Advice Bureaux.

National Federation of Housing Associations
30–2 Southampton Street, London WC2.

Age Concern: England
60 Pitcairn Road, Mitcham, Surrey.

Some Major Housing Associations in England
Abbeyfield Society
35a High Street, Potters Bar, Herts.

Anchor Housing Association
    13–15 Magdalen Street, Oxford.
Church Army Housing Ltd
    Welford House, 112a Shirland Road, London W9.
Hanover Housing Association
    Hanover House, 168 High Street, Egham, Surrey.
Jephson Housing Association
    5–7 Dormer Place, Leamington Spa, Warwickshire.
Royal British Legion Housing Association
    35 Jackson Court, Hazlemere, High Wycombe, Bucks.
World Property Housing Trust
    Prospect House, Wyllyatts Manor, Darkes Lane, Potters Bar, Herts.

Funds and Associations which run Residential Homes include:

The British Red Cross Society
    9 Grosvenor Crescent, London SW1.
The Church Army Sunset and Anchorage Homes
    Independents Road, Blackheath, London SE3.
The Civil Service Benevolent Fund
    Watermead House, Sutton Court Road, Sutton, Surrey.
Distressed Gentlefolks Aid Association
    Vicarage Gate House, Vicarage Gate, London W8.
The Friends of the Elderly and Gentlefolks Help
    42 Ebury Street, London SW1.
Jewish Welfare Board,
    315–17 Ballards Lane, London N12.
Methodist Homes for the Aged
    11 Tufton Street, London SW1.
Mutual Households Association
    Cornhill House, 41 Kingsway, London WC2.
The Religious Society of Friends
    Friends House, 173–7 Euston Road, London NW1.
The Royal British Legion
    48 Pall Mall, London SW1.
Royal United Kingdom Beneficent Association (RUKBA)
    6 Avonmore Road, London W14.
Salvation Army Women's Social Services
    280 Mare Street, Hackney, London E8.

Salvation Army Men's Social Services
   110–12 Middlesex Street, London E1.
S.O.S. Society
   14 Culford Gardens, London SW3.
Women's Royal Voluntary Service
   17 Old Park Lane, London W1.

Religious Organizations' Homes
Application for admission to one of these homes should be
made to the charity or religious organization concerned.
Charges vary and some offer shared rooms which are cheaper.
Subsidies may be requested from the local authority.
   Information on organizations which run homes can be ob-
tained from:

All religious denominations:

   The Salvation Army, 110–12 Middlesex Street, London E1
   (men's services) or 280 Mare Street, Hackney, London E8
   (women's services).

Members of the Church of England:

   Church Information Office, Church House Bookshop,
   Great Smith Street, London SW1.

Members of the Catholic Church

   The Catholic Directory

Jews

   Jewish Welfare Board, 315–17 Ballards Lane, London N12.

Members of the Methodist Church

   Methodist Homes for the Aged, 11 Tufton Street, London
   SW1.

Other sources of information:

   The Annual Charities Digest;
   Old people's welfare organizations;
   Counsel and Care for the Elderly.

Obtaining Information on Accommodation

According to interest, belief and circumstances, the following are useful sources of information:

Abbeyfield Society (housing for single elderly people);

Age Concern;

Catholic Housing Aid Society;

Counsel and Care for the Elderly;

Cyrenians (run small houses for single homeless people in need of support);

Guideposts Trust Ltd (group homes for the mentally ill);

House of St Barnabas in Soho (temporary home with a limited number of beds);

Jewish Welfare Board (provides accommodation for adults recovering from mental illness and also has residential homes for those in need);

National Federation of Housing Associations;

National Free Church Women's Council (maintains homes and flatlets in many parts of England and South Wales);

Nightingale House Home for Aged Jews;

Royal Star and Garter Home for Disabled Sailors, Soldiers and Airmen (all ages);

S.O.S. Society (runs residential homes and hostels for the elderly and people undergoing mental rehabilitation);

Sue Ryder Foundation (provides continuing care for elderly people and those with cancer as well as physically handicapped persons and those who have been mentally ill);

Thistle Foundation (provides housing and medical treatment for disabled people and their families in Scotland);

Voluntary Service Housing Association (gifted housing scheme for retired people).

The Times has also published a list of 'Homes for the Old', which is obtainable from its Features Department on receipt of a stamped self-addressed envelope (size at least 9″ x 7″).

ORGANIZATIONS

Organizations for People with Specific Disabilities and Diseases

The Chest, Heart and Stroke Association publishes excellent leaflets and will answer individual queries.

For those affected by Parkinson's disease (and their families) there is the Parkinson's Disease Society which among other activities and information services, publishes two booklets *Parkinson's Disease: A Booklet for Patients and their Families* and *Parkinson's Disease: Day to Day*.

A twenty-four hour and seven-day week counselling service is run by 'Action for Research into Multiple Sclerosis' (ARMS).

The Amandus Club helps ex-patients (mostly Parkinsonian and 'stroke' patients) to adjust to their new situation.

The Arthritic Association and the Arthritis and Rheumatism Council for Research (ARC) runs a general information and advisory service.

Also helpful are:

the Asthma Research Council;

the British Association for Rheumatology and Rehabilitation;

the British Diabetic Association;

the British Heart Foundation;

the British League against Rheumatism;

Cancer Aftercare and Rehabilitation Society;

the Cardiac Spare Parts Club (which helps patients throughout the waiting time *before* operations and assists them with problems involved in adjusting to life afterwards);

the Committee for the Promotion of Angling for the Disabled;

the Disabled Christians Fellowship;

the Disabled Drivers Association;

the Disablement Income Group;

the Equipment for the Disabled (publishes a series of a dozen illustrated booklets);

the Garden Club (for disabled people who live at home

there is a 10 per cent reduction on tools, and small grants are made available to redesign a 'difficult' garden);

Gardens for the Disabled Trust;

the Greater London Association for Initiatives in Disablement (GLAID) (its projects include self-employment schemes as well as projects to educate the public about disability);

the Greater London Association for the Disabled (works towards improvement in the quality of life of disabled people and publishes a directory of clubs in London for the physically disabled);

Handihols (provides a register of names of families who will exchange homes, often adapted for specific disabilities);

Holidays for the Disabled;

the Jewish Association for the Physically Handicapped;

Motability (voluntary organization aimed to help disabled drivers use their mobility allowance to lease a new car or to buy another through their hire-purchase scheme);

the Multiple Sclerosis Society of Great Britain and Northern Ireland;

the Muscular Dystrophy Group of Great Britain;

the National Association of Swimming Clubs for the Handicapped;

Nought to Ninety (sells aids for elderly and disabled people);

Photography for the Disabled;

Possum Users Association (assists severely disabled people);

the Riding for the Disabled Association;

the Rivermead Out-Patient Clinic for Sexual Problems of the Disabled;

the Scottish Council on Disability;

the Scottish Information Service for the Disabled;

the Scottish Paraplegic Association;

the Scottish Sports Association for the Disabled;

the Scottish Trust for the Physically Disabled;

Sesame (encourages drama for physically and mentally handicapped people);

Share Community Ltd (assists disabled people and others by providing operational training/rehabilitation projects in work and life-skills based on self-help techniques);

the Spinal Injuries Association;

the Wales Council for the Disabled;

the Winged Fellowship Trust (provides holidays in Essex, Nottingham and Sussex for severely handicapped people).

Wireless for the Bedridden (supplies free radio and television to housebound and aged poor people).

In addition, local branches of Age Concern, Help the Aged, the Citizens Advice Bureau, the Red Cross, St John Ambulance, the St Andrew's Ambulance Association (Scotland) and the Womens Royal Voluntary Service also offer various forms of advice, information and practical service. Enquiries should be made to them direct.

Organizations for Deaf Persons

Lip-reading classes are sometimes run by the local education authority and particulars of these can be obtained from the local town hall, social services department, the local Centre for the Deaf or from the British Association of the Hard of Hearing. If there are any difficulties locally, one can write to the National Council for Social Workers with the Deaf or to the Royal National Institute for the Deaf. The British Deaf Association and the British Association of the Hard of Hearing will also be able to give information on local services, clubs and societies. There are, for instance, branches of the British Deaf Drivers' Association throughout the country while the Council for Hearing-Impaired Visits and Exchanges (CHIVE) will provide exactly that service. The Commonwealth Society for the Deaf also exists to give help and advice, according to interest, locality, belief or need. The following are additional sources of assistance: the Jewish Deaf Association; the Link Centre for Deafened People (runs rehabilitation courses for people who become deaf as well as for their families); the Scottish Association for the Deaf; the Scottish Chess and Draughts Association of the Deaf. Sesame is an organization which encourages elderly people, including the deaf and blind, to take an active part in drama and so help them to produce music, movement, mime and simple acting. It works through hospitals and other relevant organizations.

Organizations Concerned with the Partially-sighted or Blind

The following have been set up to supply and assist with the particular needs of partially-sighted or blind people:

The Association for the Education and Welfare of the Visually Handicapped;

the Association of Blind and Partially Sighted Teachers and Students;

the Blind Employment Factory (makes baskets, brushes and mats);

the Braille Chess Association;

the Braille Correspondence Club;

the British Wireless for the Blind Fund (provides wireless sets for registered blind people resident in the UK and Northern Ireland);

Calibre (cassette library of recorded books);

the Free Tape Recorded Library for the Blind;

the Greater London Fund for the Blind;

the Guide Dogs for the Blind Association;

the Guild of Blind Gardeners;

the Incorporated Association for the General Welfare of the Blind;

the International Glaucoma Association;

the Jewish Blind and Physically Handicapped Society;

the Jewish Blind Society (also provides services to partially-sighted Jewish people);

the London Association for the Blind (provides training departments, workshops and residential accommodation in some areas);

the National Association of Industries for the Blind and Disabled;

the National Federation of the Blind in the UK (encourages self-help and acts as a pressure group);

the National League of the Blind and Disabled;

the National League of the Blind of Ireland;

the National Library for the Blind;

the National Listening Library;

the National Mobility Centre for the Blind (trains sighted persons as orientation and mobility instructors of the blind);

the Partially-Sighted Society (exists to meet the special needs of partially-sighted people including their educational needs);

Projects by the Blind Ltd (runs centres where visually handicapped and sighted people can join together in recreational and educational activities);

the Royal London Society for the Blind;

the Royal National Institute for the Blind;

St Dunstan's for Men and Women Blinded on War Service;

the Scottish Braille Press;

the Scottish National Institute for the War Blinded;

the Southern and Western Regional Association for the Blind;

the Sports Club for the Blind;

Talking Books for the Handicapped;

Tape Programmes for Blind people;

the Tape Recording Service for the Blind (provides facilities to have letterpress material recorded on to tape or cassette. If own tapes are used, there is no charge);

the Torch Trust for the Blind (provides Christian Braille, Moon and large print literature, talking books and cassettes as well as running a holiday home in Sussex);

the Voluntary Braille Transcribers Group in Wiltshire, a group of voluntary braillists who will teach braille to sighted persons so that they can produce braille for blind people.

Some National Organizations which will give General Information and Advice

A number of national organizations have arisen since the end of the Second World War to argue the case for improvement and to provide facilities to help old people, since their social and economic circumstances are less favourable than those of people in middle and younger years. The three main ones, Age Concern, the Centre for Policy on Ageing and Help the Aged, all have similar aims: to see old people 'respected, involved, giving as well as getting, and full and active members of the community'. Local or national offices should be contacted for advice on many issues ranging from meals services, housing, social clubs and heating to visiting and preparing for discharge from hospital. Volunteers help old people to claim their rights to adequate incomes and advise on benefits to which they are entitled.

Age Concern prepare reports on the needs of the old and present them to local and central government, and commer-

cial and voluntary organizations so that the views of elderly
people are known and can be acted upon. The four national
Age Concern bodies, in England, Scotland, Wales and Northern Ireland, brief MPs to make sure that the interests of old
people are upheld in any legislation that may affect them.
They scrutinize all measures being considered by Parliament
which relate to pensions, social security benefits, taxation,
transport, heating and housing. They are therefore in an
excellent position to give information and advice. Their publication, 'Your Rights', is a most useful guide to social security
and is kept up to date.

Help the Aged campaigns to secure better conditions and
rights for old people, issuing statements and reports. Its newspaper, *Yours*, gives much useful information. In addition, Help
the Aged offers a direct service of advice to individuals on
personal problems.

The Centre for Policy on Ageing is the new name for an
organization established in 1947 as the National Corporation
for the Care of Old People. Its aim now, as then, is to promote
better services for elderly people, 'by encouraging clearer
thinking on social policy issues'. It has become a centre for
research, advice and information, serving both policy makers
and professional people working for elderly people in this
country. Their Home Advice service gives assistance on management and improvement of homes run by voluntary organizations or by private individuals. It also issues a series of
broadsheets on topics such as nutrition and finance.

Other Sources for Advice

The social security system, like the country's health service,
is very complex. The Citizens Advice Bureaux (address of the
local bureau will be in the telephone directory) will help with
financial problems but the social workers and health visitors
have considerable knowledge of services and benefits available. If there is a physical disability the Disablement Income
Group will offer help with complicated financial problems.
The Disabled Living Foundation and the Royal Association
for Disability and Rehabilitation (RADAR) can advise where
disabilities and problems of daily living are involved. Local
social security offices also have a staff whose job it is to give
advice and disseminate information.

Bank managers provide an advisory service for financial affairs including income tax problems. If the old person does not have an account it may be worth opening one at a Trustees Savings Bank. Managers of these also offer advice on financial matters. Staff of the Inland Revenue should be contacted if the problem is connected with income tax.

Other Sources of Financial Help
The Frederick Andrew Convalescent Trust gives grants to professional women to help with convalescence. Friends of the Clergy Corporation offers financial help to the clergy of the Anglican Church, their widows and their dependants; the Society for the Relief of Distressed Widows provides some help for widows in difficult circumstances who live within five miles of Charing Cross. There are several associations and groups who are able to give help if one meets specific criteria of this kind. While the Charity Commissioners themselves are unable to supply lists of organizations who will provide this kind of help, their Central Register of Charities (in the Haymarket, London) is open for six hours every weekday and will supply names and addresses.

APPENDIX 2

ADDRESSES OF SOME AGENCIES AND ORGANIZATIONS

Addresses are given to us to conceal our whereabouts.

'Reginald in Russia' from *Cross Currents*
H. H. Munro 'Saki' 1910

NATIONWIDE LIST OF USEFUL ADDRESSES

(Some organizations deal only with correspondence and no telephone number is given in those instances.)

Abbeyfield Society
   35a High Street, Potters Bar, Herts. Tel: (77) 43371.
Action for Research into Multiple Sclerosis (ARMS)
   71 Grays Inn Road, London WC1. Tel: 01–568 2255 (N. Ireland Tel: Bangor 63378).
Age Concern: England
   Bernard Sunley House, 60 Pitcairn Road, Mitcham, Surrey. Tel: 01–640 5431.
Age Concern: Northern Ireland
   128 Great Victoria Street, Belfast 2. Tel: Belfast 45729.
Age Concern: Scotland
   33 Castle Street, Edinburgh 2. Tel: 031–225 5000/1.
Age Concern: Wales (also National Council for the Elderly in Wales)
   1 Park Grove, Cardiff. Tel: (0222) 371566.
Alcoholics Anonymous
   P.O. Box 514, 11 Redcliffe Gardens, London SW10. Tel: 01–352 9779.
Amandus Club
   31 Copse Hill, Wimbledon, London SW20. Tel: 01–946 7711. Ext. 133.
Anchor Housing Association
   13–15 Magdalen Street, Oxford.
Arthritic Association
   19 Manning Avenue, Highcliffe, Dorset. Tel: (04252) 3106.
Arthritis Care
   6 Grosvenor Crescent, London SW1. Tel: 01–235 0902/5.
Arthritis and Rheumatism Council for Research in Great Britain and the Commonwealth(ARC)
   8–10 Charing Cross Road, London WC2. Tel: 01–240 0871.

Association of Blind and Partially-Sighted Teachers and Students
c/o BM, Box 6727, London WC1.

Association of Disabled Professionals
The Stables, 73 Pound Road, Banstead, Surrey. Tel: (25) 52366.

Association for Dysphasic Adults
c/o Cicely Northcote Trust, 37a Royal Street, London SE1. Tel: 01–261 1959.

Association for the Education and Welfare of the Visually Handicapped
East Anglian School, Church Road, Gorleston, Gt Yarmouth. Tel: (0493) 62399.

Association of Inner Wheel Clubs in Great Britain and Northern Ireland
51 Warwick Square, London SW1. Tel: 01–834 4600.

Association of Jewish Refugees in Great Britain
8 Fairfax Mansions, Finchley Road, London NW3. Tel: 01–624 9096.

Asthma Research Council
12 Pembridge Square, London W2. Tel: 01–229 1149.

Beth Johnson Foundation
Parkfield House, 64 Princes Road, Hartshill, Stoke-on-Trent. Tel: (0782) 44036.

Biddle Engineering Co. Ltd
103 Stourbridge Road, Halesowen, West Midlands. Tel: 021–550 7326.

Birmingham Tapes for the Handicapped Association
20 Middleton Hall Road, King's Norton, Birmingham. Tel: 021-459 4874.

Blind Employment Factory
252–64 Waterloo Road, London SE1. Tel: 01–928 6623.

J. H. Bounds Ltd
Stethos House, 68 Sackville Street, Manchester. Tel: 061–236 7331.

Braille Chess Association
128 Walm Lane, London NW2. Tel: 01–452 8336.

Braille Correspondence Club
Specialist Officer for the Blind, Special Unit, Social Services Dept., Room 53, Civic Centre, Barras Bridge, Newcastle-upon-Tyne. Tel: Day (0632) 28520 Ext. 6320. Evening (02074) 2546.

Wales: 51, Brynifor Estate, Mountain Ash, Mid. Glamorgan. Tel: (0443) 472939.

British Association of the Hard of Hearing
   16 Park Street, Windsor, Berks.
British Association of Retired Persons
   14 Frederick Street, Edinburgh 2. Tel: 031-225 7334.
British Association for Rheumatology and Rehabilitation
   c/o Royal College of Physicians, 11 St Andrew's Place,
London NW1. Tel: 01–468 2641.
BBC Publications
   35 Marylebone High Street, London W1. Tel: 01–580 5577
British Council for Aid to Refugees
   Bondway House, 3–9 Bondway, London SW8. Tel: 01–582
6922.
British Deaf Association
   38 Victoria Place, Carlisle. Tel: (0228) 20188.
British Deaf Drivers Association
   140 Green Lane, Leeds. Tel: (0532) 672570.
British Diabetic Association
   10 Queen Anne Street, London W1. Tel: 01–323 1531.
British Gas Home Service Department
   Home Service Adviser, Marketing Division, 326 High Hol-
born, London WC1. Tel: 01–242 0789.
British Geriatrics Society
   Bernard Sunley House, 60 Pitcairn Road, Mitcham, Sur-
rey. Tel: 01–648 3596.
British Heart Foundation
   57 Gloucester Place, London W1. Tel: 01–985 0185.
British Home and Hospital for Incurables
   Crown Lane, Streatham, London SW16. Tel: 01–670 8261.
British Homoeopathic Association
   27a Devonshire Street, London W1. Tel: 01–935 2163.
British League Against Rheumatism
   c/o The Arthritis and Rheumatism Council, Faraday
House, 8–10 Charing Cross Road, London WC2. Tel: 01–240
0871.
British Library of Tape Recordings for Hospital Patients
   12 Lant Street, London SE1. Tel: 01–407 9417/8.
British Limbless Ex-Servicemen's Association
   Frankland Moore House, 185–7, High Road, Chadwell
Heath, Essex. Tel: 01–590 1124.
British Pensioners and Trade Union Action Committee
   138 Stoke Road, Slough, Berks.

British Red Cross Society
  9 Grosvenor Crescent, London SW1. Tel: 01–235 5454.
British Society for Music Therapy
  48 Lanchester Road, London N6. Tel: 01–883 1331.
British Society for Research on Ageing
  The Biology Department, Queen Elizabeth College,
London W8.
British Sports Association for the Disabled
  Hayward House, Ludwig Guttman Sports Centre, Harvey
Road, Aylesbury, Bucks. Tel: (0296) 27889.
British Talking Book Service for the Blind
  Mount Pleasant, Wembley, Middlesex. Tel: 01–903 6666.
British United Provident Association (BUPA)
  Provident House, Essex Street, London WC2. Tel: 01–353
9451
British Wireless for the Blind Fund
  226 Great Portland Street, London W1. Tel: 01–388 1266
Calibre
  Wendover, Aylesbury, Bucks. Tel: (0296) 623119.
Campaign for the Homeless and Rootless (CHAR)
  27 John Adam Street, London WC2. Tel: 01–839 6185.
Cancer Aftercare and Rehabilitation Society
  Lodge Cottage, Church Lane, Timsbury, Bath. Tel: (0761)
70731.
Cancer Information Association
  2nd Floor, Marygold House, Carfax, Oxford.
Cancer Research Campaign
  2 Carlton House Terrace, London SW1. Tel: 01–930 8972
Cardiac Spare Parts Club
  c/o National Westminster Bank, 2 High Street, Olney,
Bucks. Tel: (0234) 711181.
Carr-Gomm Society
  36 Gomm Road, London SE16. Tel: 01–237 8204/2318.
Carters (J and A) Ltd
  Alfred Street, Westbury, Wilts. Tel: (0373) 822203.
Catholic Housing Aid Society
  189a Old Brompton Road, London SW5. Tel: 01–373 4961.
Central Register of Charities
  St Alban's House, 57 Haymarket, London SW1.
Centre on Environment for the Handicapped
  126 Albert Street, London NW1. Tel: 01–267 6111.

Centre for Policy on Ageing
    (formerly National Corporation for the Care of Old People),
    Nuffield Lodge, Regents Park, London NW1. Tel: 01–722 8871.
Chariot Transport for the Disabled (Midlands)
    17 Wood Lane, Streetly, Sutton Coldfield, West Midlands. Tel: 021–353 3057.
Charles Bullen Ltd
    3–7 Moss Street, Liverpool 6. Tel: 051–207 6995.
Chest, Heart and Stroke Association
    Tavistock House North, Tavistock Square, London WC1. Tel: 01–387 3012.
Church Army Sunset and Anchorage Homes
    Independents Road, Blackheath, London SE3.
Cicely Northcote Trust
    Northcote House, 37a Royal Street, London SE1. Tel: 01–261 1959.
Citizens Rights Office
    1 Macklin Street, Drury Lane, London WC2. Tel: 01–405 5942/4517.
Civil Service Benevolent Fund
    Watermead House, Sutton Court Road, Sutton, Surrey.
Clos-o-mat (GB) Ltd
    2 Brooklands Road, Sale, Cheshire. Tel: 061-973 1234.
College of Speech Therapists
    6 Lechmere Road, London NW2.
Colostomy Welfare Group
    38–9 Eccleston Square, London SW1. Tel: 01–828 5175.
Committee for the Promotion of Angling for the Disabled
    10 Chapel Court, Thistle Foundation, Niddrie Mains Road, Edinburgh 16. Tel: 031-661 2494.
Commonwealth Society for the Deaf
    83 Kinnerton Street, London SW1. Tel: 01–235 8182/3.
Community Service Volunteers
    237 Pentonville Road, London N1. Tel: 01–278 6601.
Compassionate Friends
    25 Kingsdown Parade, Bristol. Tel: (0272) 47316.
Conservation Society
    12a Guildford Street, Chertsey, Surrey. Tel: (09328) 60975.
Consumers' Association
    14 Buckingham Street, London WC2. Tel: 01–839 1222

Contact
  15 Henrietta Street, Covent Garden, London WC2. Tel: 01–240 0630.
Contenta Surgical Trading Company
  Grove Estate, Dorchester, Dorset. Tel: (0305) 66001.
Council for Hearing-Impaired Visits and Exchanges (CHIVE)
  c/o Central Bureau for Educational Visits and Exchanges, Seymour House, Seymour Mews, London W1. Tel: 01–486 5101.
Council for Music in Hospitals
  340 Lower Road, Little Bookham, Surrey. Tel: (31) 58264.
Council of Social Services for Wales
  Llys Ifor, Crescent Road, Caerphilly, Mid-Glamorgan. Tel: (0222) 869224.
Counsel and Care for the Elderly (also Old People's Information Service) 131 Middlesex Street, London E1. Tel: 01–621 1624.
Country Cousins
  98 Billingshurst Road, Broadbridge Heath, Horsham, West Sussex. Tel: (0403) 65188/61960.
Crossroads Care Attendant Scheme Trust
  11 Whitehall Road, Rugby, Warwickshire. Tel: (0788) 61536.
Cruse: National Organization for the Widowed and their Children
  Cruse House, 126 Sheen Road, Richmond, Surrey. Tel: 01–940 4818/9047.
Cultural Society of the Disabled
  10 Warwick Row, London SW1.
Cyrenians
  13 Wincheap, Canterbury, Kent. Tel: (0227) 51641.
A. C. Daniels
  41 New Cavendish Street, London W1. Tel: 01–935 4175.
DAS Legal Expenses Co. Ltd
  Phoenix Assurance Co. Ltd, Phoenix House, Redcliff Hill, Bristol. Tel: (0272) 294941.
Department of Health and Social Security
  Disablement Services Branch, 3 Government Buildings, Warbreck Hill Road, Blackpool, Lancs.
Department of the Environment
  Building 3, Victoria Road, South Ruislip, Middx.
Dermalex Pressure Area Care Products
  146–54 Kilburn High Road, London NW6. Tel: 01–624 4686.

Dial for Help
   300 Stamford Street, Ashton-under-Lyne, Tameside. Tel:
061-339 2345.

Disabled Christians Fellowship
   Prince's Hall, 53 Prince Street, Bristol. Tel: (0272) 25694.

Disabled Drivers Association
   Ashwellthorpe Hall, Ashwellthorpe, Norwich, Norfolk. Tel:
(050841) 449.

Disabled Drivers Motor Club Ltd
   9 Park Parade, Gunnersbury Avenue, London W3. Tel:
01–993 6454

Disabled Living Foundation
   346 Kensington High Street, London W14. Tel: 01–602
2491.

Disabled Motorists Federation
   15 Rookery Road, Tilston, Malpas, Cheshire. Tel: (08298)
373.

Disablement Income Group
   Attlee House, Toynbee Hall, 28 Commercial Street,
London E1. Tel: 01–247 2128/6877.

Distressed Gentlefolks Aid Association
   Vicarage Gate House, Vicarage Gate, London W8. Tel:
01–229 9341.

Docklands Settlements
   Headquarters Offices, East Ferry Road, London E14.

Dorebridge Travel for Disabled People
   6 Shepherd Street, Mayfair, London W1. Tel: 01–493 4020.

Downs Surgical Ltd
   Church Path, Mitcham, Surrey. Tel: 01–648 6291. New
Cavendish Street, London W1. Tel: 01–486 3611.

Elbeo Ltd
   Lenton Lane, Nottingham.

Electricity Council
   30 Millbank, London SW1.

Employment Fellowship
   Drayton House, Gordon Street, London WC1. Tel: 01–387
1828.

Equipment for the Disabled
   2 Foredown Drive, Portslade, Brighton. Tel: (0272) 419327.

Ex-Services War Disabled Help and Homes Department
   (Joint Committee of St John of Jerusalem and the British

Red Cross Society) 6 Grosvenor Crescent, London SW1. Tel: 01–235 7131.

Faculty of Homoeopathy
2 Powis Place, Gt Ormond Street, London WC1.

Film Society for Disabled People
Flat Office, York Community Council, 10 Prior Street, York. Tel: (0904) 38467.

Forces Help Society and Lord Roberts Workshop
122 Brompton Road, London SW3. Tel: 01–585 3243.

Frederick Andrew Convalescent Trust
c/o Andrew and Co., St Swithin's Square, Lincoln.

Free Tape Recorded Library for the Blind
26 Laggan Road, Maidenhead, Berks. Tel: (0628) 20014 (evenings).

Friends of the Clergy Corporation
27 Medway Street, London SW1. Tel: 01–222 2288.

Friends of the Elderly and Gentlefolks Help
42 Ebury Street, London SW1. Tel: 01–730 8263.

Gardens for the Disabled Trust and Garden Club
Headcorn Manor, Headcorn, Kent. Tel: (0622) 890360.

Gardner's Trust for the Blind
Oldebourne House, 46–7 Chancery Lane, London WC2. Tel: 01–242 2287.

Gelulose Incontinency Products Ltd
91a King Street, Southport, Merseyside.

Gimson and Co. Ltd (Stairlifts)
Vulcan Road, Leicester. Tel: (0533) 21425/27272.

GRACE
P.O. Box 71, Cobham, Surrey. Tel: (09326) 2928/5765.

Greater London Association for Initiatives in Disablement (GLAID)
Flat 4, 188 Ramsden Road, Balham, London SW12.

Greater London Association for the Disabled
1 Thorpe Close, London W10. Tel: 01–960 5799.

Greater London Citizens Advice Bureaux Service Ltd
31 Wellington Street, London WC2. Tel: 01–379 6841.

Greater London Fund for the Blind
2 Wyndham Place, London W1. Tel: 01–723 1677.

A. W. Gregory and Co. Ltd
Glynde House, Glynde Street, London SE4. Tel: 01–690 3437.

Guide Dogs for the Blind Association
9–11 Park Street, Windsor, Berks. Tel: (07535) 55711.

Guideposts Trust Ltd
   74 High Street, Witney, Oxon. Tel: (0993) 72885.
Guild of Aid for Gentle People
   10 St Christopher's Place, London W1. Tel: 01–935 0641.
Guild of Blind Gardeners
   c/o Royal National Institute for the Blind, 224 Great Portland Street, London W1. Tel: 01–388 1266.
Hand Crafts Advisory Association for the Disabled
   103 Brighton Road, Purley, Surrey. Tel: 01–668 1411.
Handihols
   12 Ormonde Avenue, Rochford, Essex. Tel: (0702) 548257.
Hanover Housing Association
   Hanover House, 168 High Street, Egham, Surrey. Tel: 01–873–5461.
Hanover (Scotland) Housing Association Ltd
   36 Albany Street, Edinburgh 2. Tel: 031–557 0598.
Hartmann Fibre Ltd
   Kirk House, Birkheads Road, Reigate, Surrey. Tel: (74) 49241.
Health Education Council
   78 New Oxford Street, London WC1. Tel: 01–637 1881.
Help the Aged
   32 Dover Street, London W1. Tel: 01–499 0972.
Hetherington Charities for Aged Blind Persons
   Christ's Hospital, 26 Great Tower Street, London EC3. Tel: 01–626 6407.
Hearing Aid Council
   40a Ludgate Hill, London EC4.
Holidays for the Disabled
   12 Ryle Road, Farnham, Surrey. Tel: (0252) 716509.
Home Nursing Supplies Ltd
   Headquarters Road, West Wilts Trading Estate, Westbury, Wilts.
Horder Centre for the Arthritics
   Crowborough, Sussex. Tel: (08926) 4141.
House of St Barnabas in Soho
   1 Greek Street, London W1. Tel: 01–437 1894 or 457 5508.
Ileostomy Association of Great Britain and Ireland
   First Floor, 23 Winchester Road, Basingstoke, Hants. Tel: (0256) 21288.
Income Tax Payers Society
   40 Doughty Street, London WC1. Tel: 01–405 8662.

Incorporated Association for the General Welfare of the Blind
   8–22 Curtain Road, London EC2. Tel: 01–247 2405.
International Glaucoma Association
   King's College Hospital, Denmark Hill, London SE5. Tel:
01–274 7222 ex. 2453.
In Touch
   BBC Publications, P.O. Box 234, London NW1.
Invalid Care Allowance Unit
   Central Office, Norcross, Blackpool.
Invalids-at-Home
   23 Farm Avenue, London NW2.
Izal Ltd
   Thorncliffe, Chapeltown, Sheffield.
Jephson Housing Association
   5–7 Dormer Place, Leamington Spa, Warwickshire.
Jewish Aged Needy Pension Society
   59 Valley Drive, London NW9. Tel: 01–204 5050.
Jewish Association for the Physically Handicapped
   15 Greenfield Gardens, London NW2. Tel: 01–455 8997.
Jewish Blind Society
   1 Craven Hill, London W2. Tel: 01–262 3111
Jewish Blind and Physically Handicapped Society
   118 Seymour Place, London W1. Tel: 01–262 2003.
Jewish Deaf Association
   90 Cazenove Road, London N16. Tel: 01–806 6147.
Jewish Welfare Board
   315–17 Ballards Lane, London N12. Tel: 01–446 1499.
J. H. Bounds Ltd
   Stethos House, 68 Sackville Street, Manchester. Tel: 061–
236 7331/4.
John Bell and Croyden
   50 Wigmore Street, London W1. Tel: 01–935 5555
John Grooms Association for the Disabled (Holidays)
   10 Gloucester Drive, Finsbury Park, London N4. Tel: 01–
802 7272.
Kanga Hospital Products
   P.O. Box 39, Bentinck Street, Bolton.
Keep Fit Association
   70 Brompton Road, London SW3. Tel: 01–584 3271/7555.
Keromask Clinic for Cosmetic Camouflage
   Innoxa, 14 Porchester Place, London W2. Tel: 01–723
2509.

Kingston Trust
  The Drove, Kempshott, Basingstoke, Hants. Tel: (0256) 52320.
Legal Aid Offices
  Birmingham: Podium, Centre City House (Smallbrook Queensway), 5 Hill Street, Birmingham 5. Tel: 021–632 6541.
  Brighton: 9–12 Middle Street, Brighton. Tel: (0273) 27003.
  Bristol: Whitefriars, Block C, Lewins Mead, Bristol. Tel: (0272) 214801.
  Cambridge: Leda House, Station Road, Cambridge. Tel: (0223) 66511.
  Cardiff: Arlbee House, Greyfriars Road, Cardiff. Tel: (0222) 388971.
  Chester: North West House, City Road, Chester. Tel: (0244) 315455.
  Leeds: City Hall, New Station Street, Leeds. Tel: (0532) 442851.
  Liverpool: Moor House, James Street, Liverpool. Tel: 051–236 8371.
  London: 29–37 Red Lion Street, London WC1. Tel: 01–405 6991.
  Manchester: Pall Mall Court, 67 King Street, Manchester 60. Tel: 061–832 7112.
  Newcastle-upon-Tyne: 18 Newgate Shopping Centre, Newcastle-upon-Tyne. Tel: (0632) 23461.
  Nottingham: 5 Friar Lane, Nottingham. Tel: (0602) 412424.
  Reading: Crown House, 10 Crown Street, Reading, Berks. Tel: (0734) 589696.
Leonard Cheshire Foundation
  7 Market Mews, London W1. Tel: 01–499 2665.
Life Begins at 50
  (see Pre-Retirement Choice)
Link Centre for Deafened People
  c/o Princess Alice Memorial Hospital, Eastbourne, Sussex. Tel: (0323) 638230.
London Association for the Blind
  14–16 Verney Road, London SE16. Tel: 01–732 8771.
London Council of Social Service
  68 Chalton Street, London NW1.
London Homes for the Elderly
  94–116 Southwark Park Road, London SE16. Tel: 01–237 5802.

London Tourist Board
  26 Grosvenor Gardens, London SW1.
Loxley Medical Supplies Ltd
  Bessingby Industrial Estate, Bridlington, North Humberside. Tel: (0262) 75356.
Marie Curie Memorial Foundation
  124 Sloane Street, London SW1. Tel: 01–730 9157.
Martin Creasey Rehabilitation
  89 Clumber Street, Hull. Tel: (0482) 445229.
Mastectomy Association
  1 Colworth Road, Croydon, Surrey. Tel: 01–654 8643.
Mecanaids Ltd
  St Catherine Street, Gloucester. Tel: (0452) 418451.
Medic-Alert Foundation
  9 Hanover Street, London W1. Tel: 01–499 2261.
Medic Bath Ltd
  Ashfield Works, Hulme Hall Lane, Manchester 10. Tel: 061–205 7495/6.
Medimail
  P.O. Box 12, Bishop's Stortford, Herts.
Mediscus Products Ltd
  Westminster Road, Wareham, Dorset. Tel: (09295) 6311.
Mental After Care Association
  Eagle House, 110 Jermyn Street, London SW1. Tel: 01–839 5953.
Mental Health Foundation
  8 Wimpole Street, London W1.
Methodist Homes for the Aged
  11 Tufton Street, London SW1.
Metropolitan Society for the Blind
  252 Waterloo Road, London SE1. Tel: 01–928 1141.
Meyra Rehab (UK)
  4 Cophead Lane, Warminster, Wilts. Tel: (0985) 215122.
MIND (The National Association for Mental Health)
  22 Harley Street, London W1. Tel: 01–637 0741.
  Northern Office: 155–7, Woodhouse Lane, Leeds. Tel: (0532) 453926.
  Welsh Office: 7 St Mary Street, Cardiff.
Molnlycke Ltd,
  Southfields Road, Dunstable, Beds. Tel: (0582) 600211.

Mortgage Brokers Association
  Corporation of Mortgage, Finance and Life Assurance
Brokers, 34 Rose Street, Wokingham, Berks.
Motability
  The Adelphi, John Adams Street, London WC2. Tel: 01–
839 5191.
Multiple Sclerosis Society of Great Britain and Northern Ireland
  286 Munster Road, London SW6. Tel: 01–381 4022.
Muriel Braddick Foundation
  14 Teign Street, Teignmouth, Devon. Tel: (06267) 6214.
Muscular Dystrophy Group of Great Britain
  Natrass House, 35 Macaulay Road, London SW4. Tel: 01–
720 8055.
Mutual Households Association
  Cornhill House, 41 Kingsway, London WC2.
National Association of Almshouses
  Billingbear Lodge, Wokingham, Berks. Tel: (0344) 52922/3.
National Association of Citizens Advice Bureaux
  110 Drury Lane, London WC2. Tel: 01–836 9231.
National Association of Estate Agents
  Arbon House, 21 Jury Street, Warwick.
National Association of Industries for the Blind and Disabled.
  Triton House, 43a High Street South, Dunstable, Beds.
Tel: (0582) 606796.
National Association of Swimming Clubs for the Handicapped
  4 Hillside Gardens, Northwood, Middx. Tel: (65) 27784.
National Association of Widows
  c/o Stafford District Voluntary Service Centre, Chell Road,
Stafford. Tel: (0785) 45465.
National Benevolent Fund for the Aged
  12 Liverpool Street, London EC2.
National Benevolent Institution
  61 Bayswater Road, London W2. Tel: 01–723 0021.
National Council for Social Workers with the Deaf
  Alban Deaf Association, 1 Old Bedford Road, Luton, Beds.
National Council for the Single Woman and Her Dependants
  29 Chilworth Mews, London W2. Tel: 01–262 1451.
National Council for Voluntary Organizations
  26 Bedford Square, London WC1. Tel: 01–636 4066.
National Federation of the Blind in the United Kingdom
  20 Cannon Close, London SW20.

National Federation of Clubs for the Divorced and Separated
   13 High Street, Little Shelford, Cambridge.
National Federation of Housing Associations
   30–2 Southampton Street, London WC2. Tel: 01–240 2771.
National Federation of Old Age Pensioners Associations
   Melling House, 91 Preston New Road, Blackburn, Lancs.
Tel: (0254) 52606.
National Free Church Women's Council
   27 Tavistock Square, London W1. Tel: 01–387 8413.
National Fund for Research into Crippling Diseases
   Vincent House, Springfield Road, Horsham, W. Sussex.
National Homes Network
   Suite 303, Radnor House, 93 Regent St., London W1.
National Innovations Centre
   Bedford Chambers, Covent Garden, London WC2. Tel:
01–836 8967.
National Institute for Social Work
   Mary Ward House, 5–7 Tavistock Place, London WC1.
Tel: 01–387 9681.
National League of the Blind and Disabled
   2 Tenterden Road, London N17. Tel: 01–808 6030.
National League of the Blind of Ireland
   35 Gardiner Place, Dublin 1. Tel: Dublin 742792.
National Library for the Blind
   Cromwell Road, Bredbury, Stockport. Tel: 061–494 0217/
8/9.
National Listening Library
   49 Great Cumberland Place, London W1. Tel: 01–723
5008.
National Mobility Centre for the Blind
   22 Melville Road, Edgbaston, Birmingham 16. Tel: 021–
454 6870
National Society for Cancer Relief
   Michael Sobell House, 30 Dorset Square, London NW1.
Tel: 01–402 8125.
National Society for Clean Air
   136 North Street, Brighton, Sussex. Tel: (0273) 26313/4/5.
National Society of Non-Smokers
   Latimer House, 40–8 Hanson Street, London W1. Tel: 01–
636 9103.

Newton Aids
   Unit 4, Dolphin Industrial Estate, Southampton Road, Salisbury, Wiltshire. Tel: (0722) 20441.
Nicholls and Clarke Ltd
   Niclar House, 3/10 Shoreditch High Street, London E1. Tel: 01–247 5432.
Nicholas Laboratories Ltd
   225 Bath Road, Slough, Berks. Tel: (75) 23971.
Nightingale House Home for Aged Jews
   105 Nightingale Lane, London SW12. Tel: 01–673 3495.
Northern Ireland Council of Social Services
   2 Annadale Avenue, Belfast. Tel: Belfast 793886.
Nought to Ninety
   63 Pembroke Road, Shirehampton, Bristol. Tel: (0272) 823148.
Nuffield Nursing Homes Trust
   71–91 Aldwych, London WC2. Tel: 01–404 0601.
Officers' Association
   28 Belgrave Square, London SW1. Tel: 01–235 8112.
Officers Families Fund
   28 Belgrave Square, London SW1. Tel: 01–235 6776.
Old People's Welfare
   3 Berrylands Road, Surbiton, Surrey. Tel: 01–399 4289.
Open University
   Milton Keynes.
Optical Information Council
   Walter House, 418–22 Strand, London WC2. Tel: 01–836 2323.
Overeaters Anonymous
   c/o 182 Hutton Road, Brentwood, Essex.
Over Forty Association for Women Workers
   Mary George House, 120–22, Cromwell Road, London SW7. Tel: 01–370 2556/2507.
Over Sixties Employment Bureau
   St Albans Hall, Manor Place, London SE17. Tel: 01–703 5066.
Paintings in Hospitals
   Nuffield Foundation, Nuffield Lodge, Regent's Park, London NW1. Tel: 01–722 8871.
Parkinson's Disease Society of the UK Ltd
   81 Queen's Road, London SW19. Tel: 01–946 2500.

Partially Sighted Society
  Midlands Office, Breaston, Derbyshire. Tel: (03317) 3036.
Patients Association
  11 Dartmouth Street, London SW1.
Photography for the Disabled
  190 Secrett House, Ham Close, Ham, Richmond, Surrey.
Tel: 01–948 2342.
Possum Users Association
  14 Greenwich Drive, Timsbury, Nr Bath, Avon. Tel: (0761)
71184.
Pre-Retirement Association
  19 Undine Street, London SW17. Tel: 01–767 3225.
Pre-Retirement Choice Magazine, incorporating 'Life Begins at 50'
  Bedford Chambers, Covent Garden, London WC2. Tel:
01–876 8772.
Princess Christian Convalescent Homes for ex-servicemen
  Knaphill, Woking, Surrey.
Professional Classes Aid Council
  10 St Christopher's Place, London W1. Tel: 01–935 0641.
Projects by the Blind Ltd
  6 Castletown Road, London W14. Tel: 01–385 4211/4940.
Radio Amateur Invalid and Blind Club
  9 Rannoch Court, Adelaide Road, Surbiton, Surrey.
Riding for the Disabled Association
  Avenue 'R', National Agricultural Centre, Kenilworth,
Warwickshire. Tel: (0203) 56107.
*Rivermead Rehabilitation Centre (Out-patient Clinic for Sexual Prob-
lems of the Disabled)*
  Rivermead Hospital, Abingdon Road, Oxford. Tel: (0865)
40321.
Robinson and Sons Ltd
  Marketing Services, Wheat Bridge Mills, Chesterfield. Tel:
(0246) 31101.
Rotary International in Great Britain and Ireland
  Sheen Lane House, Sheen Lane, London SW14. Tel: 01–
878 0931
Royal Air Force Benevolent Fund
  67 Portland Place, London W1. Tel: 01–580 8343.
Royal Association for Disability and Rehabilitation (RADAR)
  25 Mortimer Street, London W1. Tel: 01–637 5400.
Royal Association in Aid of the Deaf and Dumb
  27 Old Oak Road, Acton, London W3. Tel: 01–743 6187.

Royal British Legion
  48 Pall Mall, London SW1.
Royal British Legion Housing Association
  35 Jackson Court, Hazlemere, High Wycombe, Bucks.
Royal Hospital and Home for Incurables (Putney and Brighton)
  West Hill, Putney, London SW15. Tel: 01–788 4511/2/3.
Royal London Society for the Blind
  105–9 Salusbury Road, London NW6. Tel: 01–624 8844.
Royal Medical Benevolent Fund
  24 Kings Road, Wimbledon, London SW19. Tel: 01–540 9194.
Royal National Institute for the Blind
  224 Great Portland Street, London W1. Tel: 01–388 1266.
Royal National Institution for the Deaf
  105 Gower Street, London WC1. Tel: 01–387 8033.
Royal Society for the Prevention of Accidents (ROSPA)
  Cannon House, The Priory, Queensway, Birmingham 4. Tel: 021–233 2461.
  1 Grosvenor Crescent, London SW1. Tel: 01–235 6889.
Royal Society of Health
  13 Grosvenor Place, London SW1. Tel: 01–235 9961.
Royal Star and Garter Home for Disabled Sailors, Soldiers and Airmen
  Richmond Hill, Richmond, Surrey. Tel: 01–940 3314.
Royal UK Beneficent Association (RUKBA)
  6 Avonmore Road, London W14. Tel: 01–602/6274.
Saga Holidays for Disabled People
  119 Southgate Road, Folkestone, Kent. Tel: (0303) 30321.
St Andrew's Ambulance Association
  Milton Street, Glasgow 4. Tel: 041–332 4031.
St Christopher's Hospice
  51–53 Lawrie Park Road, Sydenham, London SE26. Tel: 01–778 9252.
St Dunstan's (For Men and Women Blinded on War Service)
  P. O. Box 58, 191 Old Marylebone Road, London NW1. Tel: 01–723 5021.
St John Ambulance Association and Brigade
  1 Grosvenor Crescent, London SW1. Tel: 01–235 5231.
St John's S.O.S. Talisman
  P. O. Box 999, Kettering, Northants.
St Joseph's Hospice
  Mare Street, Hackney, London E8. Tel: 01–985 0861.

Salvation Army
   110–12 Middlesex Street, London E1 (men); 280 Mare
   Street, Hackney, London E8 (women).
Samaritans
   17 Uxbridge Road, Slough. Tel: Slough (75) 32713.
Scottish Association for the Deaf
   Moray House, Holywood Road, Edinburgh 8. Tel: 031–
   556 8137.
Scottish Braille Press
   Craigmillar Park, Edinburgh 16. Tel: 031–667 6230.
Scottish Chess and Draughts Association of the Deaf
   4 Tarfield Avenue, Woodside, Aberdeen. Tel: (0224) 44286.
Scottish Council of Social Service
   18–19 Claremont Crescent, Edinburgh 7. Tel: 031–556
   3882.
Scottish Council on Disability
   18–19 Claremont Crescent, Edinburgh 7. Tel: 031–556
   3882.
Scottish Development Department
   3 Lady Lawson Street, Edinburgh.
Scottish Home and Health Dept.
   St Andrew's House, Regent Road, Edinburgh 1.
Scottish Information Service for the Disabled
   18–19 Claremount Crescent, Edinburgh 7. Tel: Edinburgh
   031–556 3882.
Scottish National Institute for the War Blinded
   Gillespie Crescent, Edinburgh 10. Tel: 031–229 1456.
Scottish Old Age Pensioners Association
   12 Gordon Street, Lochgelly, Fife.
Scottish Paraplegic Association
   3 Cargil Terrace, Edinburgh 5. Tel: 031–552 8459.
Scottish Sports Association for the Disabled
   Fife Institute of Physical Recreational Education, Viewfield
   Road, Glenrothes, Fife.
Scottish Trust for the Physically Disabled
   9 Wheatfield Road, Edinburgh 11. Tel: 031–225 8011.
Sesame
   Christchurch, 27 Blackfriars Road, London SE1. Tel: 01–
   633 9690.
Sexual and Personal Relationships of the Disabled (SPOD)
   The Diorama, 14 Peter Place, London NW1. Tel: 01–486
   9823.

SHARE Community Ltd
  170 Kingston Road, Merton Park, London SW19. Tel: 01–542 6241.
Smith and Nephew (Southalls) Ltd
  Alum Rock Road, Birmingham. Tel: 021–327 0204.
Society for the Assistance of Ladies in Reduced Circumstances
  Lancaster House, 25 Hornyold Road, Malvern, Worcs.
Society for the Relief of Distressed Widows
  175 Tower Bridge Road, London SE1. Tel: 01–407 7585.
Society of Skin Camouflage
  Wester Pitmenzies, Auchtermuchty, Fife.
Society of St Vincent de Paul
  24 George Street, London W1.
S.O.S. Society
  14 Culford Gardens, London SW3. Tel: 01–584 3717.
Southern and Western Regional Association for the Blind
  32 Old Queen Street, London SW1. Tel: 01–222 8843.
Spinal Injuries Association
  5 Crowndale Road, London NW1. Tel: 01–388 6840.
Sports Club for the Blind (Greater London)
  3 Westlands Terrace, Balham, London SW12. Tel: 01–673 4010.
Success after Sixty
  40–1 Old Bond Street, London W1. Tel: 01–629 0672.
  33 George Street, Croydon, Surrey. Tel: 01–680 0858.
  7 Mackenzie Street, Slough. Tel: (75) 36827.
Sue Ryder Foundation
  Sue Ryder Home, Cavendish, Suffolk. Tel: (0787) 280252.
Sundial Society for Cultural Pursuits for the Elderly
  3 Perrycroft, Windsor, Berks.
Talking Books for the Handicapped
  49 Great Cumberland Place, London W1. Tel: 01–723 5008.
Talking Newspaper Association of the UK
  130 Chester Road, Watford, Herts. Tel: 01–954 6111.
Tape Programmes for Blind People
  31 Fortescue Road, Paignton, S. Devon. Tel: (0803) 522873.
Tape Recording Service for the Blind
  48 Fairfax Road, Farnborough, Hants. Tel: (0252) 47943.

Task Force
  1 Thorpe Close, off Cambridge Gardens, London W10. Tel: 01–960 5666.
Teachers Benevolent Fund
  Hamilton House, Mabledon Place, London WC1. Tel: 01–387 2442.
Telephones for the Blind Fund
  Mynthurst, Leigh, Reigate, Surrey. Tel: (0293) 862546.
Charles F. Thackray Ltd
  Viaduct Road, Leeds. Tel: (0532) 31862.
D. B. Thomas and Son Ltd
  164 Chrisp Street, London E14. Tel: 01–987 1131.
The Times 'Homes for the Old List'
  Features Dept, The Times, P.O. Box 7, New Printing House Square, Gray's Inn Road, London WC1.
Thistle Foundation
  27a Walker Street, Edinburgh 3. Tel: 031–225 7282.
Torch Trust for the Blind
  Torch House, Hallaton, Market Harborough, Leics. Tel: (085889) 301.
Travel Well
  Disabled Peoples Travel, Carlisle House, 8 Southampton Row, London WC1. Tel: 01–405 9481.
Ulverscroft Large Print Books
  The Green, Bradgate Road, Anstey, Leics.
Urinary Conduit Association
  36 York Road, Denton, Manchester. Tel: 061–336 8818.
Vernon Carus Ltd
  Penwortham Mills, Preston, Lancashire. Tel: (0772) 744493/8.
Voluntary Braille Transcribers Group
  4 Spreenwater Cottages, Old Hollow, Mere, Wiltshire. Tel: (0747) 860573.
Voluntary Service Housing Association
  43 Great Windmill Street, London W1. Tel: 01–439 3456.
Wales Council for the Blind
  Oak House, The Bulwark, Brecon, Powys. Tel: (0874) 4576.
Wales Council for the Disabled
  Llys Ifor, Crescent Road, Caerphilly, Mid-Glamorgan. Tel: (0222) 869224/5/6.

Western Provident Association
  Culver House, Culver Street, Bristol. Tel: (0272) 23495.
Wider Horizons
  Ghyll Cottage, Ings, Kendal, Cumbria. Tel: (0539) 821274.
Widows Association of Great Britain
  56 Gainsborough Road, Grindon, Sunderland, Tyne and Wear. Tel: (07834) 2556 and (0632) 853868.
Widows Friend Society
  Nasmith House, 175 Tower Bridge Road, London SE1.
Winged Fellowship Trust (Holiday Centres)
  64–6 Oxford Street, London W1. Tel: 01–636 5575/5886.
Wireless for the Bedridden
  81b Corbets Tey Road, Upminster, Essex. Tel: 01–865 0051.
Women's Holiday Fund
  125 Wilton Road, London SW1. Tel: 01–834 4743.
Women's League of Health and Beauty
  66 Downscourt Road, Purley, Surrey. Tel: 01–660 5256.
  2 Rosebery Gardens, London W13. Tel: 01–997 9524.
Women's National Cancer Control Campaign
  1 South Audley Street, London W1. Tel: 01–499 7532/4.
Women's Royal Voluntary Service
  17 Old Park Lane, London W1. Tel: 01–499 6040.
Workers' Educational Association
  Temple House, 9 Upper Berkeley Street, London W1. Tel: 01–402 5608/9.
World Property Housing Trust
  34 High Holborn, London WC1. Tel: 01–405 6783.

REFERENCES

Age Concern, *Why Do People Mumble so Much?* Age Concern 1978.

Age Concern, *Retirement Move – Longer than a Holiday.* Age Concern 1978.

Argyle, Michael and Beit-Hallahmi, Benjamin, *The Social Psychology of Religion.* Routledge and Kegan Paul 1975.

Baker, A. A., 'Slow Euthanasia or She'll be Better Off in a Hospital' (*British Medical Journal* No. 2 1976), pp. 571–2.

Baker, J. Austin, *The Foolishness of God.* Darton, Longman and Todd 1970.

Bell, Donald, *Crime Prevention.* Age Concern and National Westminster Bank 1980.

Bergman, Shimon, *Ageing in a Forming Society – Implications for Research Teaching and Social Policy for Ageing in Israel.* Tel Aviv University 1977.

Berkowitz, 'Informed Consent: Research on the Elderly' (*The Gerontologist.* vol. xviii, no. 3 1978).

Binks, F. Allen, 'Changing the Subject' (*Lancet.* July 1 1978).

Blyth, Alan, 'Music Reviews' (*Daily Telegraph* 4 June 1980 and 11 June 1980).

Bowder, Bill, *Ageing in the Eighties.* Age Concern 1980.

Bradbury, Sue, Covering letter to all members of the Folio Society with the Prospectus for 1979–80.

Brearley, P., 'Understanding Risk' (*Social Work Today.* vol x, no 31 3 April 1979).

Brocklehurst, J., 'Ageing and Health' in *The Social Challenge of Ageing* (ed. David Hobman) Croom Helm 1979.

Browne, R., 'The Old Need Cure not Compensation' (*Community Care* no 259 12 April 1979).

Centre for Policy on Ageing, *Homes Advice*, Centre for Policy on Ageing 1980.

Claydon, Stella, 'Images of Age' in *Liberation of the Elders* (ed. Sidney Jones) Beth Johnson Foundation Publications in Association with the University of Keele 1976.

Clough, Roger, 'No-one could call me a fussy man' (Social Work Today, vol ix, no 34, 2 May 1978).

Collins, Joan, *The Joan Collins Beauty Book*. Macmillan 1980.

Davies I., and Schofield J. D., 'Theories of Ageing' (ed. J. C. Brocklehurst) *Textbook of Geriatric Medicine and Gerontology*. Churchill Livingstone 1978.

Dickson, Niall, *Living in the 80's: What Prospects for the Elderly?* Age Concern 1980.

Duncan, A. S., et al. *Dictionary of Medical Ethics*. Darton, Longman and Todd 1977 and 1981.

Eliot, T. S., 'Burnt Norton' *The Four Quartets*. Faber and Faber 1938.

Erikson, E., *Insight and Responsibility*. Faber and Faber 1964.

Franks, H., 'A Death without Dignity' (The *Guardian* 5 May 1979.

Gaine, Michael, 'Ageing and the Spirit in the Social Challenge of Ageing' (ed. David Hobman) Croom Helm 1979.

Garden, Jackie, 'Solving the Transport Problems of the Elderly: the use of Resources'. Beth Johnson Foundation Publications in association with the University of Keele 1978.

Glendenning, Frank, (ed.) 'Self-Help and the Over-60's'. Beth Johnson Foundation Publications in association with the University of Keele and Age Concern 1978.

Gray, Muir, 'Forcing Old People to leave their Homes' (*Community Care* 8 March 1979).

Gray, Muir, and Mackenzie, Heather, *Take Care of Your Elderly Relative*. George Allen and Unwin and Beaconsfield Publications 1980.

Grenfell, Reggie, and Garnett, Richard, (eds.) *Joyce – by Herself and Her Friends*. Macmillan 1980.

Gutman, G. M., and Herbert C. P., 'Mortality Rates among Relocated Extended Care Patients' (Journal of Gerontology vol xxxi, no 3 1978) pp. 352–7.

Havighurst, Robert, 'Ageing in Western Society' in *The Social Challenge of Ageing*. (ed. David Hobman) Croom Helm 1979.

Huxley, Aldous, *Brief Candles*. Triad Panther 1977.

Johnson, Stevens, and Reed, *The Complete Works of William Shakespeare with Biographical Sketch* 1890.

Jones, Sidney, 'Education for the Second Half of Life'. *Living in the 80's: What prospects for the elderly?* Age Concern 1980.

Jones, Sidney, 'Liberation of the Elders', Beth Johnson Foundation Publications 1976.

Jung, C. G., *Four Archetypes*. Routledge 1962.

Macartney, P. *Clothes Sense for Handicapped Adults of All Ages*. Disabled Living Foundation 1973.

MacDonald-Wallace, J., 'Health Education for Better Living in Later Years' *Liberation of the Elders* (ed. Sidney Jones) Beth Johnson Foundation in association with the University of Keele 1976.

Maclean, Sir Fitzroy, *Tito: A Pictorial Biography*. Macmillan 1980.

Maddox, Brenda, 'It can be Fun at 50' 'Observer Living' (*The Observer*. 10 August 1980).

Mandelstam, Dorothy, *Incontinence: A Guide to the Understanding and Management of a Very Common Complaint*. Heinemann Health Books 1977.

Marris, Peter, 'Conservatism, Innovation and Old Age' (Unpublished Paper) University of California, Los Angeles.

Maslow, A. H., *Motivation and Personality*. New York, Harper and Row 1970.

Masters, John, *The Field Marshal's Memoirs*. Sphere 1979.

Moberg, D. O., 'Religiosity in Old Age' (*The Gerontologist*. vol v, 1965) pp. 78–87.

Norman, Alison, 'Rights and Risks' (Discussion Document on Civil Liberty in Old Age). The Centre for Policy on Ageing 1980.

Priestley, J. B., and Hawkes, Jacquetta, *Journey Down a Rainbow*. Penguin 1969.

Quiller-Couch, Sir Arthur, (ed.) *The Oxford Book of English Verse 1250–1918*. Oxford University Press 1957.

Raphael, Winifred, and Mandeville, J., *Old People in Hospital*. King Edward's Hospital Fund for London 1979.

Rhodes, Margaret, and Webber, Ann, *Street Warden Schemes: Action Guide*. Age Concern 1976.

Richards, Tom, Hospital After Care Schemes: Action Guide. Age Concern 1980.

Richards, Tom, *Transport Schemes: Action Guide*. Age Concern 1978.

Rogers, Dorothy, *On Stage for the Over 60's*. Age Concern 1978.

Rowse, A. L., 'As Old as you Feel' (*Daily Telegraph* 13 September 1989).

Rubin, S. G., and Scott-Samuel, A. J. R., 'When Community Care Fails' (*Health and Social Service Journal*. 10 January 1976).

Rubinstein, Artur, *My Many Years*. Cape 1980.

Sheldon, J. H., 'The Effect of Age in the Control of Sway' (*Gerontologia Clinica* vol v 1963) pp. 129–38.

Sheldon, S. Tobin, 'The Educator as Advocate: The Gerontologist in an Academic Setting': *Journal of Education for Social Work*. Vol ix, no 2 1973) pp. 94–98.

Smithson, John, *Practical Help Schemes: Action Guide*. Age Concern 1980.

Thomas, Lewis, *The Lives of a Cell, Notes of a Biology Watcher*. Bantam Books 1975 and 1979.

Thomas, Lewis, *The Medusa and the Snail. More Notes of a Biology Watcher*. New York, Viking Press 1979.

Tournier, Paul, *Learning to Grow Old*. S.C.M. 1972.

Wavell, A. P., *Other Men's Flowers*. Cape 1944.

West, Morris, *The Ambassador*. Heinemann 1965.

Whitehead, Tony, 'Ageing and the Mind' in *The Social Challenge of Ageing* (ed. David Hobman). Croom Helm 1979.

World Health Organisation, *The Third Age*. World Health Organisation April 1979.

INDEX

ability, improving *see* function
accidents 13, 94, 109–11; *see
    also* risks
addresses of organizations
    187–209
advice, organizations for 183–5
Age Concern 28, 183–4, 189;
    on callers 112; and
    community care 111; and
    housing 35, 46, 49, 54, 61,
    108; and leisure 49, 87; and
    medical help 11, 113,
    115–16, 118, 121, 127–8; and
    mobility'87, 123–5
ageing process 3–29; and body
    12–16; and dependence
    132–72; and emotions 17–18;
    and independence,
    maintenance of 31–133; and
    mind 16–17; and ourselves
    3–9; and science 10–18;
    social and economic
    background to 18–29
aid: financial 148, 185; legal
    74–5; summoning 113–14
aids 110–11, 128–33, 149;
    centres 131–3; clothing
    124–5, 130–1; cooking 124;
    hearing 115–17; heating 107;
    incontinence 127–8, 130,
    153–7; mobility 123–5; sight
    118–19; *see also* organizations
alarms 112–13
allowances 22, 46, 67–74
almshouses 52
Alvin, J. 84
Anderson, F. 98
annuities 63–4, 66–7
appearance 90–3, 152

Argyle, M. 166, 210
attendance allowance 71–2

Baker, A. 139, 210
banks 64, 185
Beckett, S. 20
Beit-Hallahmi, B. 166, 210
benefits 22, 46, 67–74
bereavement *see* death
Bernanos, G. 165
Berridge, B. 85
Blake, W. 19
blind 14–15, 117–19; aids for
    118–19; organizations for
    182–3
Blyth, A. 81, 210
body: ageing 12–16;
    appearance of 90–3, 152;
    exercise of 12–13, 90, 99,
    103, 108–9, 180
Böhm, K. 81–2
Booth, C. 81
Bowder, B. 28–9, 210
Bradbury, S. 104, 210
Brearley, P. 138, 210
breathing problems 14, 95,
    159–61
Bridges, R. 81
Brocklehurst, J. 12, 210
Browne, R. 115, 210
Browning, E. B. 163
Bryant, Sir A. 81
building societies 40–1, 64, 66
buying a home 40–1

capital: investment 63–6;
    transfer tax 76–7
care: foster 50; shared 50;
    skilled 147–50

Casals, P. 82
Centre for Policy on Ageing 55, 61, 183–4
Chichester, Sir F. 82
Churchill, W. 81
Citizen's Advice Bureaux 175; and housing 45–6, 49, 61, 63, 107–8, 110; legal and financial advice 74–5, 77, 168, 170; and leisure 87; medical advice 121
Claydon, S. 19, 210
clothing 92–3, 106, 124–5, 130–1
Clough, R. 143–4, 210
club life 49–50
colostomy 131
communications development 25
companionship 161–2
cooking 101–2, 124; *see also* food
cosmetics 91–2
council *see* local authority
crime 111–14

Davies, I. 11, 211
de Gaulle, C. 80
deafness 15, 115–17; 181
death and bereavement 163–72; after funeral 170–2; attitudes to 163–6; care for dying 146–62; certificate 167; fear of 147; funeral 169–70; grant 170; in institutions 140–1; registration 168–9; statutory responsibilities 166–70; of tenant 46
dementia 17, 141
dentures 101, 120–1
dependence, acceptance of 132–72; bereavement 163–72; care for ill and dying 146–62; risks and rights 137–45
depression 47–8, 122, 140, 171–2; *see also* mental health
development in third age 5–6

Dickens, C. 173
Dickson, N. 89, 211
diet 15, 99–103, 106–7, 150–2
disabled: benefits for 73–4; organizations for 101, 110, 124–5, 129–31, 148, 179–84
disease: organizations for 179–81; prevention of 33
Disraeli, B. 87
dying *see* death

Ecclesiastes 63
economic and social background to ageing 19–29
education 5, 27, 82–7; health 97–9
Eliot, T. S. 172, 211
emotions and ageing 17–18
employment 21–3, 26, 88–90
Erikson, E. 20, 211
exercise 12–13, 90, 99, 103, 108–9, 180; *see also* mobility

faecal incontinence 127, 153
famous people, longevity of 79–82
fear of death 147
Fields, W. C. 103
financial affairs 62–77: aid 148, 185; annuities 63–4, 66–7; banks 64, 185; benefits and allowances 22, 46, 67–74; building societies 40–1, 64, 66; grants 35–9, 45, 107, 170; insurance 75–6; investment 63–6; loans 66–7; taxes 76–7; wills 77–8
fire, danger of 109–10, 138
food and drink 15, 99–103, 106–7, 150–2
foster care 50
friends, living with 47–9
Fry, C. 137
fuel crisis 23–4
function, restoration of 114–29;

aids 128–33; dentures 120–1; hearing 115–17; incontinence 125–7; memory 121–3; mobility 123–5; sight 117–19; speech 119–20
funerals 169–72; *see also* death

Gaine, M. 165, 211
gerontology 10–11
Gibbon, E. 31
giddiness 14
Gladstone, W. 81
government securities 64
granny annexe 51–2
grants: death 170; improvements and repairs 35–9, 45, 107
grief 47–8, 166, 171
grooming *see* appearance
group living 50–1
Gutman, G. M. 48, 211

hallucinations 62, 171
Hardy, Sir A. 8
Harwood, E. 84
Havighurst, R. 23–4, 211
health 11, 93–114; diet 99–103; education 97–9; exercise 103, 108–9; in institutions 140–1; mental 104–5; promotion of 96–9; risks and rights 109; safety 109–11; warmth 105–9, 158
hearing loss *see* deafness
heating 105–9, 158
Help the Aged 183–4
Herbert, C. P. 48, 211
Hobbes, T. 81
home buying 40–1
homes, old people's 54–61, 176–8; *see also* living
Horace 2
hospitals *see* institutions
hotel accommodation 52
housing associations 54, 57, 60, 175–8; *see also* living

Huxley, A. 3, 163, 211
hygiene 149, 152, 156–7
hypothermia 105–9

ICA *see* invalid care allowance
ileostomy 131
ill and dying, care for 146–62
illness insurance 76
Illyes, G. 8, 211
improvements and repairs 35–9, 45, 107
income *see* allowances; financial affairs; pensions
incontinence 125–7, 152–7; aids 127–8, 130, 153–7
independence: maintaining 31–133; in financial and legal affairs 62–77; health 93–113; improving ability 114–32; living arrangements 33–62; oneself, continuing to be 78–92
industrial disablement and injuries benefit 73
information: revolution 28–9; sources 173–85
Inge, Dean 81
injury: benefits 73–4; insurance 76; by others 111–14
inquest 168
institutions, life in 54–61, 138–45, 175–8
insurance 75–6; company loans 41
intellectual deterioration 16–17; *see also* mental health
invalid care allowance 72
investment 63–6

James, W. 8
Jones, S. 83–6, 211
Jung, C. G. 21, 211

Koyl, L. 24

landlord's responsibilities 44–5

laundry 156–7
law centres 74
laws: health 138–9, 141, 144: housing 42–6; *see also* statutory
learning *see* education
leasehold property 45
legal affairs 74–8; advice and aid 74–5; insurance 75–6; obligations 166–70; taxes 76–7; wills 77–8
leisure 26, 80, 87–90, 104–5, 179–80
Levin, B. 7–8
liberty *see* rights and risks
life insurance 75
listening 146–7
literature, influence of 19–21
living arrangements 33–62; almshouses 52; clubs 49–50; foster care 50; granny annexes 51–2; group living 50–1; hotels 52; housing associations 54, 57, 60, 175–8; institutions 54–61, 138–45, 175–8; new patterns, settling to 61–2; old people's homes 54–61, 176–8; organizations for 138–45, 175–8; owner-occupiers 36–41; relatives and friends 47–9; shared care 50; sheltered housing 53–4; tenants 35–6; 41–6
loans *see* financial affairs; grants
local authority housing 35, 41, 46, 53–4
loneliness 6–7, 104–5, 146
longevity 3–4, 79–82
love 7, 90

Macartney, P. 130, 212
MacDonald-Wallace, J. 96, 212
Macmillan, H. 81
make-up 91–2
Marris, P. 47–8, 79, 212

Masefield, J. xiv–v, 146
Maslow, A. H. 20, 212
Masters, J. xiv, 7, 212
maturity loans 66
medical organizations 49, 88, 102, 129–33, 145, 148–50, 152, 178–81
memory loss 6, 16–17, 121–3
mental health 6, 97, 104–5; depression 47–8, 122, 140, 171–2
mind, ageing 16–17
mobility: aids 123–5, 180; allowance 72–3; and exercise 12–13, 90, 99, 103, 108–9; loss of 105, 122–5
money *see* financial affairs
Montaigne, M. E. de 94, 135
mortgage 40–1; annuities 66–7
Mulford, J. 85
Munro, H. H. 187
Murdoch, I. 145

National Giro 65
National Savings Bank 65
new pattern of living 61–2
Norman, A. 79, 137, 139, 141, 143, 212
nursing homes 60–1

occupation pension 68
odour control 157
old people's homes 54–61, 176–8
oneself, continuing to be 78–92; appearance and body 90–3; education 82–7; love 90; recreation 87–8; work 88–90
Open University 27, 86, 104
organizations 173–85; addresses of 187–209; disablement and disease 101, 110, 124–5, 129–31, 148, 179–84; housing 138–45, 175–8; medical care 49, 88, 102, 129–33, 145, 148–50, 152, 178–81

ourselves and the ageing
  process 3–9
over-80s pension 68–9
owner occupiers 35–41

pain, freedom from 148–9
Payne, J. H. 33
pensions 22, 67–9; *see also*
  financial affairs
personality 17, 34, 97
Plato 9
Pope, P. 61
population projections 19
possession insurance 75–6
Post Office savings 65
post-mortem 167
Poulden, S. 84
private facilities 56–7, 76, 150
probate 78

radio 27
rebates 46
recreation *see* leisure
refusal to grow old 4–5
relations, living with 47–9
religion: and death 147, 161,
  165; and residential care 177;
  revival of 27–8
rented accommodation 35–6,
  41–6
repairs, home 35–9, 45, 107
residential care 54–61, 138–45,
  176–8
retirement 6, 87–8; and
  employment 21–3; pension
  67; preparation for 83–4
rights and risks 109, 137–45; *see
  also* accidents
Rowse, A. L. 81, 212
Rubinstein, A. 82, 212
Russell, B. 81

safety 109–11
savings *see* investment
Schofield, J. D. 11, 211

science and the process of
  ageing 10–18; body 12–16;
  emotions 17–18; mind 16–17
security of tenure 42
selling home 39
sex and love 7, 90, 180
Shakespeare, W. 3, 20, 164
shared care 50
shares 66
Shaw, G. B. 81
Sheldon, S. T. 10–11, 213
sheltered housing 53–4
shopping, new methods 25–6
sight loss 14–15, 117–19, 182–3
skilled care 147–50
sleep 158–9
smell, sense of 15
Snagge, J. 81
social and economic
  background to ageing 19–29
social life and values 6–7
speech problems 119–20
spiritual development 7–9, 18,
  90; *see also* religion
statutory: responsibilities
  166–70; tenancy 43–4; *see also*
  laws
stress 15–16
supplementary benefits 70–1

taste, sense of 15
taxes 76–7
teeth 101, 120–1
telephone 25
television 25
tenants 35–6, 41–6
Tennyson, A. L. 81
Thomas, L. 163–4, 213
Titian 81
Tito 80
touch, sense of 15
Tournier, P. 165, 213
transport 25
trust fund mortgages 41

understanding ageing process
  10–18
unemployment 23; *see also*
  retirement

Voltaire 81
voluntary services *see*
  organizations

war disablement 73–4, 148
warmth 105–9, 158
washing aids 129
Whitehead, T. 17, 213
widows 69–70, 172
wills 77–8
Wordsworth, W. 10, 90
work 21–3, 26, 88–90